FIFTY BLOGS:
FOR READERS AND
WRITERS

Claudia Tomlinson

Book designed by Vassil Lakov

Copyright © 2017 Claudia Tomlinson

ISBN: 1-5410-9605-3
ISBN-13: 978-1-5410-9605-9

Dedicated to my son Laurence

CONTENTS

BLOGS ON COMMUNITY
AND SOCIETY

BLOGS ON ARTS AND REVIEWS

BLOGS ON POLITICS AND SOCIAL COMMENTARY

Introduction

People use the word 'blog' to mean several different things, and as a result it can be difficult to pin down the exact meaning. Mostly, it is understood as an article or piece of short, punchy, succinct, mostly prose writing, designed to bring to the attention of others.

The term can also be used to describe the place where blogs are published, such as a website established by an individual, or a team, to curate and publish their own blog articles or those of others. The owner of such blog websites also act as editors.

People can run websites purely for their own blogs and do not offer the opportunity for any interaction or input from others. Bloggers can also include any type of content on their blogs including poetry, images, short stories, videos, podcasts and any other outputs or offshoots from the blog.

So, content can range from very technical data, to the most creative and visual information.

People do not tend to write blogs for their own personal consumption as they might do with a diary or journal. The purpose of posting or publishing their blog pieces is to be share experiences and information with others.

The popularity of a blog does relate to the subject of the blog, the popularity of the blogger, the publication in which the blog appears, and the overall success of the blog. Success can be measured in a number of ways, including number of people reading and interacting with the material, how often it is shared, and it can also be measured in financial terms if the blog has been monetised.

Why blog?

The reasons why people decide to start blogging usually falls into three main categories, for business, personal and professional reasons.

Business blogging

Blogging is important in business as a platform for establishing a community of people who share the values, interest and perspective of the blog.

Blogs can be established on a business model, with income generation as the core purpose. Alternatively, blogs can be established for personal or professional reasons, with the option to monetise them at a later stage.

Using a planned business model, the opportunities for the blogger are unlimited, and there are many examples of well-established blogs using a clear business model. The best example is probably Darren Rowse's Problogger which shows the unlimited business potential of a blog to develop and expand over many years.

A successful business blog can offer opportunities in books, podcasts, public speaking, classroom and virtual courses, workshops, advertising and affiliate marketing.

Despite the mushrooming of microblogging sites, video and live-streaming, image and multimedia messaging apps, the place held by traditional blogging remains important. Blogging is very useful as a stand-alone entrepreneurial tool, as well as a platform for interacting with audiences through other media and social media.

Personal blogging

Because blogs are often the vision of a single person, at least at start, they are most typically the personal perspective of an individual. Many are established by individuals to share their opinions with a like-minded community. This community can be of people who share a passion such as sport, a political perspective, a hobby or special interest such as fashion, beauty or cookery. It can also be a community of people who have a shared experience that they wish to bring out into the open such as victims of forms of injustice who can use the blog to challenge the establishment, or for whistleblowing. Blogs can also be used to share insights through personal health treatment journeys, throwing great insights into previously masked experiences.

Professional blogging

People can start blogs to create and draw together a like-minded group of professionals to form a community. With the huge growth and diversification of professional groups, and reduced expenditure of public and private funds for opportunities for face to face networking via conferences and forums, professionals are increasingly relying on virtual opportunities. There are well established blogs for a large range of professional groups including for police, prison, medical, nursing, education, social care professionals. Blogs can be run by an individual to describe their experiences and perspectives, or specifically for sharing views and opinions of the community through comments and contributions from readers.

Mixed models

The reality of blogging is that there is usually a mixture of approaches, with personal and professional blogs sometimes eventually becoming partly or wholly monetised. Some blogs are developed with a 'free' model, then gradually introduce paid for services and products, retaining a core free offer.

How to get into blogging

The first blog in this book is about getting into blogging, and making an impact. Depending on the model of blogging you choose to get into, it is possible to start straight away. If you want to publish it on an established site, there are many looking for guest bloggers. There are many lists of top blogs, most powerful blogs, best fashion blog, top sport blogs, most influential political blogs etc., and while these can be aspirational for the beginner blogger, there are many opportunities.

It is possible to set up a website and publish a first blog on the same day, depending on your technical skills, which do not need to be advanced. Many providers offer 'off the shelf' websites that are easy to customise such as Wordpress, Wix, Moonfruit etc. If you do not have the experience of building a simple website, and only want to focus your energies on creating blogs, you can outsource this task. A friend, colleague or family member may be able to help you with setting up a website, or you can outsource it to a professional. The fastest and most efficient way is to hire a virtual professional from a site such as Peopleperhour.com, Guru.com and upwork.com to hire freelancers on a world-wide basis. If you prefer, you can hire someone to work with you on a face to face basis, to design your website to your specification.

Images and multimedia

Most of my published blogs included the use of images curated by the editor or by me to illustrate the pieces. The original images have all been included in this book, but some of the images used to illustrate the blogs are shown. The use of images is an extremely important part of blogging, as images and videos bring your blogs to life. The presence of images draw people in and entice them to read the article to find out more about the message they have seen in the image.

To obtain images you need to publish those you have permission to publish. These will be photographs you have taken yourself, or have been taken on your behalf specifically for you to use. There are also several websites that provide copyright-free images for use by anyone and this is a great solution. These public domain images can be found on sites such as Flickr, Pixabay, and Pexels.

The one consideration to bear in mind is that although many thousands of images are available, the more popular ones are used often, particularly of unusual or esoteric subjects. As such, be prepared for the risk that your carefully selected images may also be adorning other popular blogs on the same topics. If this is important to you, then obtaining your own images independently is the way forward for you.

Reader comments

Blogs have a comments section which is very popular with readers who see it as a way of engaging with the subject, interacting with the writer, and other readers. This is a rewarding part of writing blogs, a way of gauging interest in a subject, which may point to demand for similar blogs. It indicates which topics bring most traffic to your blogs, which can be useful if you wish to adopt a business model.

The other side of reader comments can be dark as people can join a site specifically to troll the blogger, the topic or other readers. As mentioned before, people with opposing views can join to provide contrasting views and opinions, but that is different from trolling, which is commentary designed to cause arguments and stir up trouble in the community.

Responding to comments to blogs is generally highly recommended, it can generate more interest, engagement and sharing of the blog. Bear in mind there will always comments posted to troll, and you will have to develop a strategy to identify trolls, and whether or not to respond to them. My own strategy is to never respond to trolling comments, but you will have to decide whether there is any positive value in doing so. I include the blog comments, edited for legal reasons, to some of my blogs in this book, to show the range of comments blogs can be attract.

If re-posting or publishing reader comments, you will need to guard against liability for legal issues arising from the comments posted by readers. For this reason, some publications do not accept reader comments, or moderate them before publication.

Legalities

The standard legal obligations exist for writers of blogs as for writers of any other publication. Bloggers need to guard against defamation (libel) and copyright infringements in the production of their material. Blog websites are also obliged to ensure the blogs they accept for publication are in keeping with the law. If you have the intention of blogging as a business model this is an area to be fully scoped. Those who are professionals will also be bound by professional standards and codes of conduct that can be infringed through blogging activity. It is up to each individual blogger, sometimes with guidance from an editor, to assure themselves that they are publishing within the law.

Why write this book?

I wanted to write this book to capture the many blogs I have written over the past five years in a single place. Blogs can appear to be ephemeral as they are quickly conceived, written and published. They are consumed at a rapid rate, and moved on from. The blogs presented in this book were mostly published on well-established and respected websites of national newspapers, and highly rated blogs. The subjects were mostly conceived and developed by me, and submitted for posting or publication after review by an editor. Some, were requested by editors who wanted my perspective on a subject of new story. Others were published on my own blog websites. The book also includes unpublished material, that cannot be read elsewhere.

The book presents those interested in reading blogs with the opportunity to do so in book form, without the necessity to go online, and conduct searches.

The book will be of interest to those that share my social and political perspectives on topics that are not frequently aired in mainstream media, social media or in the blogosphere. Under-represented perspectives and voices are not often heard, including from people who are homeless, unwaged, low waged, ill, disabled particularly with mental health conditions, and people from black and ethnic minority backgrounds. The current political and economic climate, particularly in a post-Brexit era, does not bode well for the diversification of public voices.

Blogs can be a powerful campaigning tool, drawing attention to issues that the establishment ignores or covers up, and the selection of blogs I have included provides examples of many challenging issues and topics that can be covered.

Because these voices and perspectives are seldom heard, it is often to established bloggers that mainstream media go to when some of the issues explode onto the front pages, and established, mainstream journalists have no experience of the topic.

1

How To Write Successful Blogs and Become a Content Creator - Achieve Your Ambitions in 2017

Over the years, I have published blogs that have called out blatantly sexist adverts, drawn attention to the experience of women who get acid thrown in their faces to limit their life chances, and described the family psychodrama of Ed Miliband's feud with brother David. My blogs have also described the campaign to alleviate the miserable conditions of Canadian First Nations, the black miners gunned down by police in South Africa, and how a South African taxi driver was dragged to his death by a police vehicle.

I have also blogged album reviews, and interviews with bands such as the Selecter and Stone Foundation, literary review, and promoted community events such as International Women's Day and called out the rise of fast fashion. Interest in blogging remains high, people read blogs and still want to write them.

Yes, microblogging, vlogging, livestreaming, and multimedia apps have exploded in popularity, and the question is sometimes asked -surely reading blogs is old school?

Reader demographics certainly come into play with the twenty-five to sixty-four-year-old age span being the largest readers of blogs. There are readers outside this age range, for example, The Huffington Post attracts strong readership right across the age span.

To write blogs for top sites such as the Huffington Post, the Independent, and the Guardian and similar national titles, competition is strong, even for established writers with high profiles. Most of these publications need good bloggers, and are open to new voices.

A strong blogging voice, with something different to say, preferably something no one else is saying or commenting on is ideal. If you have, or can develop a personal profile that will be of interest to readers, there will be interest in you joining a blogging panel on a national site.

The starting point if you are a beginner blogger is to hone your writing skills, and strengthen your unique voice. Don't be afraid of expressing a strong or controversial opinion. Whether it is about lifestyle subjects, social or political affairs, let your unique voice ring out!

If you are a beginner, online and classroom based courses on blogging, and social media for writers are available.

Most websites that accept contributions from bloggers have contributor's guidelines. There are two main models for submitting articles as a guest blogger to a website. You may find yourself working directly with a contributions editor who you must pitch an idea to each time. The independent newspaper blogging page operates on a model of working directly with an editor, as does the Guardian's Comment is free page.

When you have a relationship with an editor, you pitch an idea in a few sentences, and if it is accepted by the editor, you are invited to develop it into a full blog and given a word limit. When you submit the full piece, expect it to be published within a day or so on the site. The editor may make changes.

The second submission model, such as used by the Huffington Post Blog, differs as once you have successfully pitched your first article you will be accepted as a member of the blogging panel or team and do not need to pitch ideas to the editor each time. You then go on to submit developed blogs, on any subject, to the blog team editors who review and check it for critical issues, and publish it, normally on the next working day.

Most websites that accept blogging see it as an opportunity for you, to raise your profile and have a marketing platform. For this reason, there is not usually a fee paid to bloggers. There are many alternative opportunities to monetise your blogging, and you can be paid to place articles. Once published, the opportunities for sharing and promoting the blog are unlimited.

The final point to bear in mind is that with most websites that publish your blog, you remain the owner of the content, the copyright is owned by you and you can re-use the content as you wish. Some publications, such as Huffington Post, retains the right to also use your content as it wishes, and that is part of the deal.

So, the potential benefits, I believe, are unlimited, whether you wish to blog as a hobby, or as an apprenticeship to a career in journalism. It is perfect if you want to pull together a community around a subject, to develop a business model, or to be a professional content creator.

As a content creator, your options are limitless. A final few words - go for it, and be bold about it.

BLOGS ON COMMUNITY AND SOCIETY

2

Even her appointment to the House of Lords can't curtail Doreen Lawrence's campaigning spirit

The UK is woefully short of authentic black voices in politics and, once in power, careerism often pulls ambitious black politicians away from their value system.

When it was announced that race equality campaigner Doreen Lawrence would be entering the House of Lords as a new Labour peer this month, there was a swirl of reactions. Grassroots campaigners who have journeyed with her since the racist murder of her son Stephen, in 1993, have feared the neutralisation of her power. How can she sustain her influence within such a reactionary British institution?

For most of us the title 'Baroness' conjures up the image of a wealthy, privileged, upper-class woman, white, and out of touch with much happening below the level of her usually long nose. Or, a rampantly forceful woman, determined and domineering, but again not showing much interest in listening to and understanding others - a bit in the mould of Baroness Margaret Thatcher.

Baronesses from ethnic minority backgrounds have not been very visible, except, like Baroness Warsi, for the wrong reasons. Sayeeda Warsi was seen by some as fodder, caught up in the Tory party spin machine, a mere token ethnic minority woman who was parachuted into the Lords. She was not viewed as having an authentic voice of the cultural community she belonged to, and was rejected by many British Asian Muslims. It is extremely unlikely that Doreen will suffer this fate, and she continues to be admired not only by ethnic minorities, but by the millions from all backgrounds that she has inspired over the past twenty years.

Many voices also have celebrated and welcomed Doreen's appointment, fully expecting that her considerable personal power will not be diminished in the Lords, and on the contrary, she will be a welcome force for change in the creaky institution.

So what will Baroness Lawrence need to do to convince her grassroots followers that she will continue in the style that is so admired: one of a quiet, but determined and dignified fighter? There will be just one expectation: that she retains her core beliefs and values. The UK is woefully short of authentic black voices in politics, and it has been argued that careerism inevitably pulls ambitious black politicians away from their value system. It is not often one hears a back bench MP or junior minister from an ethnic minority background campaigning for race equality. That is normally left to pressure groups and community leaders.

At a time when the Government is showing a lack of commitment to equality legislation, and the role of the Equality and Human Rights Commission has been substantially reduced, we need a voice like Doreen's more than ever. It is also a masterstroke of Labour, recently facing claims of taking the black vote for granted, and of failing to show commitment to robustly fighting discrimination.

There is no fear of that with Doreen, and we can be sure she will be telling anyone who addresses her as 'Baroness' to call her by her first name, she has been purely motivated by her basic belief in human rights, equality and justice. In a country that claims to be civilised, and seeks to export its democratic systems around the world, for her, injustices must be identified and rooted out. It is this belief that has led her to shine a light on, fight and overcome each new insult in her fight for justice for her son.

This year, the twentieth anniversary of the murder of her son, and only a year after finally seeing two of the killers behind bars, it is a good time for her to focus on a formal role. Her recent confirmation that allegations of racial profiling by the Government's recent arrests of suspected undocumented migrants is an issue very much on her radar, suggests that race equality remains firmly on her agenda.

We have to be assured, that this woman, who has not been silenced by institutional injustices, corrupt people and systems, and illegal procedures, will also not let the House of Lords protocols curtail her campaigning, questing flame.

3

What I See project: how asking women to look in the mirror is empowering

If seeking to promote strong self-esteem, confidence and empowerment in women, most people would start with pep talks about educational achievement, setting high career goals, avoiding or postponing commitments to family domesticity, and participating in politico-feminist activism.

Not many people would ask women to start by looking in the mirror. Promoting female focus on their visual appearance has been the root of many evils linked to the subjugation of women globally, and internationally.

For example, the No More Page 3 campaign highlights the negative societal impact of the objectification of women through use of the visual. Further, the image obsessed fashion industry stands accused of imperilling the self-esteem of normal women through selecting to depict and promote a body type that is unhealthy, and it also has questions to answer about the lack of racial diversity on international catwalks. Looking at the media, the successful legal action by Miriam O'Reilly laid bare the reason for the disappearance from our screens of experienced women media practitioners such as Moira Stewart and Selina Scott, as they aged, while their male counterparts are still going strong.

So, why is a female empowerment project asking women to look in the mirror? The What I See project aims to promote the global empowerment of women by asking them to look in the mirror. This seems counterintuitive to female empowerment, but the project was set up by entrepreneur Edwina Dunn specifically to illuminate the shadows where women's positive contributions and achievements are hidden, and amplify their voices. Despite her considerable achievements in the corporate world, as the founder of the Tesco Clubcard programme, she observed and experienced a lack of commitment to hearing the voices of women in the boardroom.

She set up 'What I See' as a not-for-profit project, as a global online platform for women to contribute their stories to inspire and motivate themselves and others. Women are asked the simple question 'when you look in the mirror what do you see?'

Now with more than 500 contributions, from women in 11 countries, participants are showing they are able to look beyond the visual. Women talk about themselves as people, their aspirations, achievements, struggles, ambitions and hopes. Contributions from women incorporate their lives in science, motherhood, politics, fashion, and sport.

Women taking part in the project have looked beyond their own visual representation and differences of ethnicity, age, disability have all been powerfully uncovered in video stories.

A clear finding of the project has been the changing themes of issues for women according to their age. The socialising effects of women's engagement with their visual appearance holds less resonance for women as they grow older and focus on their place in the world.

What about women who are unsighted, are they excluded? Indeed not, as evidenced by the contribution of Hannah, a partially sighted academic who examines other ways of being, when not reliant on the visual.

Women can also participate in the Twitter web chats using the hashtag #WISPchat to join conversations such as the recent debate about whether women are affected by Imposter Syndrome where people can be plagued with self-doubt and negative self-talk which undermines or prevents them progressing to the next step, or to value their achievements.

The possibilities for this project are exciting, as women learn from the contributions of others in the project, and then share how they use this learning to improve their lives. As the project is formally launches this month, it will continue to be available as a nurturing, online community.

4

Why I'm giving up clothes for Lent

Do we really need to restock our wardrobes so frequently?
A fashion fast could help tackle poverty wages in the industry.

Could you live with a staple wardrobe of just six items of clothing for six weeks? For example: three tops, one dress, one pair of trousers, and one pair of shoes?

In thriftier times, and in many less affluent countries today, this might constitute a respectable amount of apparel. Today, clothes still only serve a functional purpose for many people. They are merely for warmth, dryness and modesty, and often do not provide even these basics of comfort. Fortunately, the majority in this country don't have to make do in this way, because clothing in Britain is cheap, plentiful, and disposable.

However, with the growth of consumerism, clothes now need to give us all a sense of identity: to make statements about ourselves that might change from one day to the next. So, for several years now, 'fast fashion', has been on the rise. This is a race between high street brands to attract consumers by selling cheap, disposable clothing, pushing down prices, and increasing production costs, meaning that brands need to find cheap labour. Such labour is mainly sourced in poor countries such as Bangladesh, which experienced a terrible disaster last year with the collapse of the Rana Plaza garment factory, in which thousands died. Some of the British brands using cheap labour in that factory acknowledged their role and offered compensation to the families of the casualties. But not all labels have been so forthcoming, and many victims and their families have yet to receive recompense.

At this year's International Women's Rights Conference, organised by charity African Initiatives, the campaign group Labour Behind the Label will explore how fashion can change the world.

Labour Behind the Label does not support or advocate any boycott of the fashion industry, as the point is not about putting already poor workers into greater poverty by taking away their livelihoods. Instead, a fashion fast will help us think about whether we really need another little black dress or another pair of skinny jeans, and collectively we can slow down demand and the pressures on the garment factories. This will promote better pay and conditions.

As Labour Behind the Label explains: "Brands put huge pressure on factory owners to complete high orders and maintain a fast turnover, which in turn equates to factory owners pressuring garment workers to produce ever greater quantities of clothes. These are produced at poverty wages. In a bid to outdo their competitors, brands push prices down in a 'race to the bottom', and garment workers' wages remain at poverty levels, and corners are cut on factory safety, resulting in horrific tragedies."

Fashion consumerism proceeds at a rampant pace throughout the year, as elite designers, catwalk models, and their entourages glide between Paris, London, New York, and Milan. With the season of Lent almost upon us, this is also the time of year when many people start to think about giving something up, for spiritual and other reasons. Maybe you could consider a fashion fast? Wear less to give more.

5

Corporate apologies for stop and search: a sorry idea

It would be better to allow officers the powers only when they have demonstrated clear and consistent competence

Northamptonshire Police is looking at proposals to make individual police officers apologise if they use stop and search powers without justification. So is this a good idea? One that will genuinely improve relations between the police and communities as intended?

Northamptonshire's Conservative police and crime commissioner, Adam Simmonds, is right to look at this issue because of concerns about the low conversion rate between stop and search and conviction rates. Less than 10 per cent of stop and searches lead to an arrest, and in almost thirty per cent of stops there were deemed to be insufficient grounds.

That most of the public have confidence in this use of stop and search police powers, according to a YouGov study, is no justification for this continued approach, as we have a public with very conservative views on public order and justice. More worrying is the mind boggling discovery that stop and search powers have been used on 300 toddlers.

The disproportionate use of the powers against black and ethnic minority members of the community continues to give cause for concern. Simmonds is to be commended for his appointment of Duwayne Brooks, a friend of Stephen Lawrence who was with him at the time of his murder, and a former Liberal Democrat councillor, to conduct a review into stop and search for the service.

Simmonds has also introduced a sanctions initiative, where stop and search rights will be withdrawn from any officer who has inappropriately applied the power on three occasions.

The problem with the latest idea is that corporate apologies can ring very hollow, a bit like the naughty child made to say sorry to a sibling, with a parent standing over them. The apology never sounds genuine, like they really mean it, and the person receiving it knows that the naughty child is highly likely to poke their tongue out as soon as the parent goes away.

The person on the receiving end of the misdemeanour knows that they still need to watch their back when around the naughty child who has just been made to say sorry; only they will be angrier next time.

Further, the use of a three-strikes approach against officers is setting them up against the community, with its punitive approach, and pits officer against community member, which is counterproductive to the aim of achieving greater police-community relations.

The police would be better looking at the issue the other way around, and expect that officers will only be able to use the powers only after they have demonstrated clear and consistent competence. New officers, during their probationary period, will have extensive training, working closely with members of the public and communities during this period, and to a clear set of standards.

Lastly, police should also build on the initiatives many have already embarked on, around building community cohesion and greater integration. For too many, contact with the police is still solely about crime and punishment. The police are still too remote, and mutual suspicion between them and communities has not significantly shifted in recent decades.

The widening of the entrance criteria for new candidates may be a factor that contributes to greater trust, particularly with older trainees being recruited in greater numbers.

In this case, sorry is not the hardest word. Glib corporate apologies are likely to be perceived as meaningless, and indeed as adding insult to injury.

Reader comments:

 Stop and search based on profile data seems a very efficient and sensible policing method to me.

6

Acora Ltd insults women with shockingly sexist advert, then botches apology

Acora IT Outsourcing Ltd has caused shock and dismay with the publication of an advertisement that is extremely offensive and insulting. The company, which has an all male leadership team according to its website, has shown that it is completely out of touch with the fact that 1970s style sexism is no longer acceptable. The image is a visual 'joke' reminiscent of the 'comedy' of people like Bernard Manning and Jim Davidson, and it is incredible that the company thought this would amuse its clients, or the public in 2013.

Describing their vision in the following way, this is a company that has proved it is out of touch with modern social responsibility:

"We believe that thought-leadership drives innovation. We are dedicated to constant progress, sharing knowledge, and creating a valuable resource for the businesses we work with"

The decision to run with this advertisement undermines any claim to a progressive vision, or to innovation. It would be interesting to know what market research methodology was used to develop this piece of marketing, and whether it was tested its target audience, the largely male IT audience it is aimed at, or whether the general public was involved.

Following a huge backlash and much criticism, Acora Ltd tweeted a statement which amounts to nothing more than a reinforcement of the blindness that led to the publication of the advertisement in the first place.

In their 'apology' there is no recognition that the advertisement is unacceptable, instead suggesting that it is acceptable apart from some who failed to find it funny.

They have completely missed the point that there are damaging consequences of such images for everyone. Although it is a woman who is the object of ridicule, and the man is depicted in a dominant position, men often find these images demeaning of women.

Additionally, men would reject being placed a role that they do not find appealing. Contemporary men do not view their relationships with women in the light suggested by this advertisement.

The impact of such images on the education children and young people, about power in gender relationships, is destructive as it promotes a passivity-dominance model of a bygone age, but one which underpins domestic violence and abusive, unhealthy relationships.

Acora Limited has also insulted its customer base, which surely would not want to be associated with the core message underpinning this advert: IT is a sexist, misogynistic world which does not care about social progression, as long as a few sexist people are amused by the disgusting demeaning of women – and a lot of business is done.

Reader comments:

Sex with ugly people is always funny. It will always be so long as immediate sexual attraction is based on looks.

That they've done a poorly thought out ad doesn't make it the end of the world. You've overread it way too much and they should have just reversed the genders and no one would have batted an eyelid. Arguably you could read the ad as her being the sexually aggressive dominant woman and he's the plucky guy trying to figure out how to get out of it. Also the picture is a play on a classic establishing shot in film, it isn't to put him in a dominant position over her, it puts the focus centre stage, which in this case is her not him.

It doesn't insult women, unless they have no sense of perspective; all it does is upset the PC brigade, who by now should really be packing their bags and leaving the world to the grown ups

You are a man and have no clue what overreading is when insulting women! It is an offensive ad and shame on those who think sex is "funny" with or without "ugly" people. You will likely not be attractive forever and neither will your mother, your sister, your daughter in today's superficial world. Think about that!

By being offended by something like this, you are simply undermining the Progressive agenda.

 Offensive to women? Confrontational to fat people is perhaps more accurate. Sure, it's insensitive, but if this is already so horribly shocking, I wonder what hysterics will have be pulled out when something really offensive is published.

 Can I ask a simple question, Would this still be sexist if it was a man lying on a bed instead of a woman? This is clearly a joke about having relations with an unattractive person not an insult to woman. Sexism and misogyny is banded about these days far too much. I am not a sexist and believe that everyone was created equally so personally I find this advert rather funny and amusing. I shall point out one simple fact, the only people that find this sexist are the people that are sexist one way or the other.

 Yes, it would still be wrong if it were the other way round. If a person finds another unappealing for whatever reasons why are they contemplating having intimate relations with that person? This ad is portraying unhealthy attitudes towards relations between people of any gender or sexuality. I feel it would speak volumes about a persons view of their own relationships to miss that point...

 I'm a woman and don't find it offensive at all. In fact I think it's an excellent piece of marketing, it's done it's job, people are talking about it, you either love it or hate it. If you hate it don't look at it. There would not be this much fuss if it was a fat bloke on there instead of a woman.

 I agree with you Michael. People who find this sexist must also find adverts by the likes of Fairy washing up liquid adverts sexist as it always a woman washing up. Surely that's a sexist advert!

 Love the fact advertising on this site is just as sexist – stop picking on one company as its a global issue – also surely there is more pressing issues in the world on sexism

 A useful public service – an ad it has told me about Acora and that on no accounts should I hire them.

It's just disgustingly offensive. Both the advert and the apology. Acora have shown absolutely no remorse at all – if they had at least admitted that they made a judgement in error, then that would have helped things.

 I can just imagine the all male board sitting around scratching their heads.. wondering why people are kicking up a stink. It's the utter lack of diversity that means they've got no one pushing them or making them question their own thoughts and views. If this is what they think makes an effective advertising campaign, you've got to think about what they think is an effective employee and customer treatment policy. I'd hate to work there! (or be a customer).

 The ad showcases Acora's Neanderthal mind set. I am dropping them from my contact book. As a case in point, IBM has around 300K employees in India that work on a wide range of industry leading platforms and products, carry out cutting edge research and deliver world class IT consulting/services. This ad while potentially depicting Acora's values is offensive on so many levels.

 All the females that found this "offensive" must be overweight and butt ugly like" the subject"

7

Mid-Staffordshire: Why the police investigation must not target powerless NHS workers

Labour was in government during the period in which the Mid–Staffordshire NHS Foundation Trust presided over the abuse and neglect of thousands of patients, leading to many deaths.

Labour was in government during the period in which the Mid–Staffordshire NHS Foundation Trust presided over the abuse and neglect of thousands of patients, leading to many deaths.

Now, a police investigation has been launched to review between 200 – 300 deaths at the Trust, where there are clear indications of abuse and neglect. The scope for bringing criminal charges will also form part of the police review.

The publication of the report of the Francis Inquiry earlier this year found failings by the bodies charged with oversight and monitoring responsibilities and inadequate responses to the many complaints of patients and their families.

Jeremy Hunt made it clear in his comments earlier this year that he would like to see nurses, doctors and managers face criminal prosecution, noticeably leaving out MPs, Monitor, the NHS regulator, also cited by Robert Francis QC as having failed to protect patients.

It's not hard to imagine that nursing staff, among the most disenfranchised NHS workers, are very likely to find themselves in the frontline for investigation. Working for years under extremely poor conditions, nurses at the Trust felt their voices were ignored.

Cruelty, neglect and abuse cannot be excused but can be explained. It can certainly be prevented by a well-resourced and supported teams of care professionals.

Tory MP Charlotte Leslie has not wasted any time in seeking

to opportunistically score political points by calling for the tentacles of the police investigation to reach into the former Department of Health (DH), and look at the actions of the former Labour government.

It is to be assumed that Ms Leslie will similarly call for police investigation of Tory and Lib Dem politicians as part of the current NHS investigation into an excess 3000 deaths in 14 NHS trusts since 2010.

The Tories will undoubtedly seek to gain political capital out of this investigation. Overworked frontline workers and junior/middle managers may disproportionately face criminal sanctions.

However most important are the victims who were at the bottom of this pitiful pile. Mostly elderly, disempowered and vulnerable, this is an opportunity for justice for those harmed and those still suffering.

This move must be supported, but the police investigation must be independent, transparent, balanced, and above all not be stained by Jeremy Hunt's determination to gain a few votes for his Party.

Reader comments:

Let's take an analogy. Harold Shopman murdered 250 patients. Was he a 'powerless' NHS worker'? There were failures by the overseeing authorities to pick that up. Does that mean that Shipman shouldn't have been investigated? Does it mean that Shipman should only have been investigated if we also investigate the overseeing bodies? Hardly. Notice how Ms Tomlinson's article carries one of the fundamental strains of socialism that you will read over and over again on these pages: 'ordinary' working people are never to blame for anything, and are absolved from all personal responsibility, whilst 'fat cat' managers and immoral, overpaid men in suits are the cause of all the world's problems. I wonder if Ms Tomlinson's mother was left writhing in agony in her own feces and left to drink from a vase by nursing staff, whether she'd maintain such a naive, juvenile view of society.

Our son John died as result of the failures at Mid-Staffs all we have been asking for for the past seven years is the truth and for justice to be done.

 Think you will find that is different kettle of fish altogether, the point that is being raised here is that usually in cases like this those who advocate policy in the first-place escape scot free thinking everything is hunky dory and it is the people who are on the ground who are at fault. It would be me telling you to buy a large jar of milk and then feed it to the cat, however I only give you 50p and the milk is £1. The cat dies in my view I did nothing wrong as i gave you the money it is you who is at fault and so should be prosecuted. That is the problem and concerns with the system that this article is raising.

 So, it wasn't a management failure at all? I suppose it was just a bunch of psychotic nurses. I suppose we can't criticise the chaps in charge. That's 'socialism.

 It was both a management and a clinical failure. All parties should be brought to account. That includes nurses.

 Sparky, just seen this now. There's no mention of people drinking from vases in the very detailed Francis Report. I believe it comes from Julie Bailey, and it seems like Francis (who took evidence from her) disregarded it.

8

Measures must be introduced to curb the spread of acid attacks on young women

Politicians need to decide whether new legislation is required to deal with this crime before it spreads. The acid attack on model Katie Piper in 2008 was the first high profile assault of acid violence in the UK. Earlier this month, a fifteen-year-old boy was charged with an acid attack on a woman in Romford, London, and last year model Naomi Oni (pictured) suffered an acid assault also in East London. At the time of the attack on Piper, this type of crime was almost unheard of in the UK. Now, alarmingly, they appear to be on the increase.

Internationally, most victims are young women in countries such as Cambodia, India, Pakistan, Bangladesh, Nepal and Uganda, who are assaulted as revenge or punishment.

Children are also frequently victims, targeted as a mechanism of controlling and hurting their mothers.

The effect is to inflict lifelong physical and psychological injury, impacting women's future capacity for work, and to form relationships, and have partners and families of their own.

Fortunately, victims in wealthy Western countries often have the resources to secure treatment for their physical and psychological injuries. However, women in poorer countries often face total incapacity. Apart from the impact on a woman's looks, injuries frequently include visual impairment or blindness or loss of eyes. The acid, thrown into the face, is frequently swallowed causing severe oral, and throat injuries, as well as damage to hands, causing disability.

Although the trend of acid violence is increasing in the UK, there is no clear pattern of the context in which it occurs, as there is internationally. The international contexts for these attacks are family, domestic, and relationship factors, as seen in the case of Katie Piper.

There is a case for more research due to the devastating impact of this crime on individuals and families. The Winston Churchill Memorial Trust published a report by barrister Shabina Begum, on the international picture for acid violence, calling for the UK to conduct large scale research to understand the emergence of this crime in the UK.

There is a need to identify high risk victims in the UK, as it is recognized that some instances of this crime are going unreported in the UK. Identification of the source of the acid and ensure steps are taken to reduce the availability of corrosive substances.

The recent episodes involving young British women resist inevitable conclusions that this is a 'minority' problem, rather than a concern for the mainstream population.

In addition to research, politicians need to decide whether new legislation is required to deal with this crime before it spreads.

Reader comments:

 Could you post the link to the NHS Information Centre's database please? I assume it's from this website (http://www.hscic.gov.uk) but I can't find the data.

 Secular education and legal access to handguns will go a long way to solving this problem in the UK. Might help with all of the other violent crime types – never know if you are going to get shot when attempting this kind of violence.

 Because, obviously, someone will be expecting the attack, and gave a gun ready at all times? Please don't use the rise if this particular horrific crime as an excuse for a general demand for guns, as that would lead to even greater problems.

9

Why it's right to extend hate crime legislation to members of subcultures

Hate crime is when someone is targeted because the assailant hates 'what' that person is or what the assailant perceives them to be. In some quarters, there has been an expression of dismay that Manchester Police will now record criminal acts against subcultures as hate crimes, where there is evidence of this. Hate crime is when someone is targeted because the assailant hates 'what' that person is or what the assailant perceives them to be.

In some quarters, there has been an expression of dismay that Manchester Police will now record criminal acts against subcultures as hate crimes, where there is evidence of this.

Currently, legislation only recognises five characteristics as eligible for recording: race, disability, religion, sexual orientation and transgender identity.

These characteristics are mostly visible, may be what people are born with birth, or something that becomes integral to their identity later in life. People with characteristics in the existing categories have borne the brunt of hatred arising out of prejudice, discrimination, social isolation and marginalisation.

There isn't unanimous agreement that there should be some classes of hatred and criminal activity that warrant special protection in law. This view is aligned to the social antagonism against equalities and human rights legislation.

Measures intended to address inequalities, such as affording greater protection for those more vulnerable to social hatred, are often viewed suspiciously by those who are not included under the umbrella of added protection. Where there is acceptance of a further measure of protection to five classes of characteristics currently included in hate crime legislation, there is resentment at it being extended to those who are members of subcultures.

This resentment is driven by widespread hostility to people who choose visible identification with alternative, unconventional lifestyles, and choose to show this in their appearance. Suspicion of youth culture, and associating it with deviance and criminality also underlies the vulnerability to becoming victims of violent crime.

The murder of Sophie Lancaster in 2007 was the impetus for the campaign for legal protection of members of subcultures. But many argue that this is a step too far because people embracing subcultures are choosing a lifestyle that subjects them to hate and that membership of a subculture is a frivolous, passing phase, compared say to religion, and can be abandoned without serious impact on the person.

It is claimed that this waters down the notion of hate as experienced by traditional victims. The fact is, however, that a civilised society cannot claim to be so if it fails to protect those who are hated, attacked for no other reason than they outliers from the mass.

People with a propensity to wreak devastation on victims and their families through hate should face added legal sanctions if a civilised society is to be maintained. Finally, where would society be without subcultures? The most acclaimed international art, music, and film genres have emerged out of the creativity of people who whose appearances were considered deviant in their day.

Reader comments:

 If someone gets beaten up and it seems to be a random attack, the attacker will be convicted of the crime. Why should there be a different sentence if it becomes apparent that the victim went to Eton and the attacker hates people who went to Eton?

 Due to the fact that, arguably, it suggests predetermination – If the attacker chooses to discriminate between people, only attacking those who went to Eton, it's much easier to imply there was some sort of long-term dysfunctional belief and thought process behind the attack.

This is in comparison to a random attack, which could simply be seen as a more spur-of-the-moment, indiscriminate, unplanned act – obviously no better, in many cases arguably worse, but also suggesting that it's either unlikely to be repeated, or that the person is of a naturally unstable disposition and is likely to receive treatment.

Mainly, it could be seen as the difference between intent and non-intent; but I think part of it also comes down to the moral belief that people simply shouldn't be judged and discriminated against based on the virtue of their birth, development or choices in life – be that going to Eton, or identifying as a Goth.

10

Are there parallels between administrators on the high street and in the NHS?

Following the demise of Jessops and HMV, Claudia Tomlinson looks at whether there parallels between administrators on the high street and in the NHS. The UK has recently been lamenting the decline of long established high street businesses that have gone into administration, particularly in relation to the ensuing impact of job losses, and lost goods or services to customers.

The introduction of a Trust Special Administrator into the NHS in 2012 to manage the deficit at South London Healthcare was an unwelcome precedent likely to result in similar poor outcomes for the stores, its staff, and local area.

The fate of stores such as Jessops and HMV are particularly hard as their staff are part of the community and have largely been unceremoniously dumped out of the jobs, a harm that will impact their families and prospects. This has led to some desperation among Jessops's now unemployed staff. Like Jessops, the Trust Special Administrator (TSA) made a recommendation South London Healthcare NHS trust be dissolved.

However, Michael Kershaw (the special administrator) is using the process to restructure all main NHS health services in south east London, including significant reduction of emergency care and maternity services at Lewisham Hospital.

In his final report, he stated:

"The TSA has concluded that these sites cannot be made financially viable in the current service and organisational arrangements. To continue in this form would require the Trust to be sustained indefinitely by cash support from the Department of Health.

"In view of this, recommendation 5 proposes a necessary reorganisation of services across south east London."

Health secretary Jeremy Hunt and the special administrator were due to meet with local MPs to enable the former to make a decision on the report recommendations by February 1st.

What is clear from the campaign against the loss of these services from Lewisham Hospital is the primary concern is about the loss of vital health services. However, there is another layer of meaning and benefit for communities about loss of services where they had positive and memorable experiences.

It is very nice to be able to go a hospital to have your baby, which is the same place you had your previous children, and where you mother gave birth to you.

As well as changes to roles, movement to new jobs, or possible redundancies for NHS staff, and loss of services, there will be a wider impact on the community, of hospital closure or loss of key services.

Most hospitals draw a large number of volunteers from the local community, people who want to give something back and help others. Additionally, many NHS trusts have developed their own charities to provide vital funds to add enhancements to patient experience, and increasingly, important hospital equipment.

Hospital volunteers and charity fundraisers gain key benefits from pursuing their activities. Many are retired, some with disabilities or long term health conditions; some are socially isolated; and some are unemployed young people seeking experience to help them into work or further training. They act as welcomers to greet and guide anxious arriving patients; they are meal companions feeding vulnerable patients; and they are befrienders visiting isolated patients. They also perform a range of administration, and semi-skilled roles in the NHS offices, that have been progressively stripped of paid staff since 2010. For no financial reward, they are saving the NHS many millions that it would cost to pay them.

Loss of hospital departments and hospitals has a major impact on volunteers who are often in their roles for much longer than staff, and hold a lot of organisational memory.

Networks, relationships and communities, frequently described as social capital, grow up around hospitals, and are therefore put at risk at risk with closures, much in the same way as post office and high street store closures.

David Cameron is introducing a change from April 2013 to systematically ask all NHS patients whether they would recommend a service they have used to friends and family, if they need the same care or treatment. But what do these recommendations mean when an administrator is introduced to manage an NHS trust with problems and makes drastic recommendations against the interests of patients and communities?

Securing economic efficiency and sustainability in the NHS is essential, but this needs to be clearly aligned to the needs of the community. PwC, the administrator for Jessops, and Michael Kershaw, the special administrator for South London Healthcare NHS Trust, are proceeding with a business focus, not considering the broader impact or fall out of their courses of action on communities and people.

Reader comments:

But that's the problem with people like you. You don't consider all the consequences.

You've draw a boundary, and inside the boundary are all the bad or good things that you want included. Meanwhile anything else, well its not going to happen because you've excluded it, e.g. Lets take the state pension. You've taken all the contributions for state pensions, civil service pensions etc., and spent them. A lots gone on the NHS, A good thing you're claiming. What about the pensions? Its a debt, its needs to be repaid, with interest on top. What about that? Not a concern. Someone else's problem. Well the problem is that you can't pay them. All this spending has come at a cost, and the cost is no pensions will be paid. The debt is too large for the tax. The debt is too large even if you took all earnings in the UK, 100% income tax, to pay. Meanwhile, patients are being starved to death by that friendly nice, NHS. Compensation? Bugger off, you're a victim.

No, you're so wrong I don't know where to start. Spending money on a health system like the NHS saves the country money in the long run. The American equivalent Costs three times as much, and for the moment doesn't even cover everyone. Whereas the NHS is the cheapest system in Europe by any measure. Short-term savings like the closing Lewisham Hospital may seem necessary to you but consider the fact that closing the hospital will cost the taxpayer 195m and leave 750,000 people with only one A&E ward. Also, the recent refurbishments cost over 12 million and now the empty buildings will be sold for 17 million. The damage done to the NHS doesn't seem worth it to me and is probably going to cost more money down the line.

The idea that one of the biggest economies in the world can't afford basic health services for its citizens is absurd. But you're right it's about boundaries, the government doesn't mind spending billions of pounds on a reorganisation to privatise the system or lavishing tax breaks for millionaires and billionaires, and cutting corporation tax. Left foot forward is just arguing that that money could be better spent on curing sick people.

It's a right-wing myth that the Labour government overspent on health, you guys always seem to forget about the bank bailouts and the global financial recession. It's always good to put this in context, pre-credit crunch the Labour government had actually more than halved the Tory debt they inherited in 1997, and John Major ran worse deficits in 1994 than Gordon Brown in 2010 according to the IMF. It's always good to put this in context.

That's right, you object to people being treated in the first place. And yes, keep on lying about the pension. It was always intended to be funded out of current revenue. And they're not a debt, they're a liability. You're the one who is refusing to pay tax, treating it as someone else's problem. YOU are the one who is looking at our entirely normal, for a western country, pension liability and opposing paying it. Keep on killing! He objects to people not paying him for care, Danny.

And how much out of the NI have you saved for those people's pensions?

The answer is nothing. You've run up debts of 5,300 bn. A 26K a year worker could have had a fund for their retirement of 560,000 pounds if you hadn't looted it.

Meanwhile, 20-80,000 a year killed by the NHS. Negligence, starvation, wrong drugs, just plain killing. It's not a myth and you are lying though your back teeth on the reductions of state debt.

Put the numbers up. How much does the state owe for its borrowing, its PFI (Lewisham being a good example), Pensions, losses on guarantees.

If you want the context.

Bank bailouts, 30 bn, most of which was that idiot Brown buying shares in bankrupt banks. Should of let them go to the wall. So that's the loss. What about the profits? 35 bn on penal rates of interest. 220 bn of taxes in 4 years. So what about the bank bail out? Since the money has gone to the government and not the other way round, its the banks (in reality their customers), bailing out the bankrupt state. Meanwhile, what about the state finances?

1,100 bn of borrowing
5,300 bn of pensions debts
400 bn of PFI
100 bn of nuclear decommissioning
Expected losses on guarantees such as BT Pension fund, Post office pension fund, ...

[Even the customer compensation scheme is an insurance policy with premiums paid by other banks, not the state]

7,000 bn of debt for past accruals. ie. Stuff paid for up front, but not delivered, or stuff delivered with the bill still to come. So what's the context? That 7,000 bn only has 1,100 bn on the books. The rest is a pure Ponzi. So what's going to happen. You've swapped short term delivery of Lewisham, for no services in the future. You've defrauded people out of their pensions, by spending all their money and leaving a debt that can't be paid.550 bn a year won't service a 7,000 bn debt when you are spending 700 bn a year. Like a 2 year old in Sweet shop, you want it now and you will lie when it comes to paying the consequence.

It's someone else that run up the debt or ate all the sweets. Not you, even though you've chocolate plastered all over your face. Come one, tell us what you've done with people's pensions contributions? Own up that a 26K a year worker is out by 430,000. Stand up and be proud and tell them that they are going to have to go on welfare? Stand in the same room, when you have to tell them you can't pay their welfare.

Correct, it's designed to use current funds. Well done. Keep on using your fraudulent figures, thief. Keep on trying to incite people to commit violence, yet another crime, based on your fraud, Keep on arguing that healthcare for the poor is wrong. Keep on arguing that only your offshore cash deserves protection. You are determined to borrow more and more to collapse the economy, of course, so you can reduce wages and probably get slavery back, knowing your hatred of the 99%. You have poisoned the sweets out of malice, years ago. The UK government, of course, lower state pension commitments than the average European country. And try suggesting to Germany that they're bankrupt – they'd laugh in your face, and rightly so. And yes, keep on refusing to tell them yourself, coward, that you are trying to murder them. You can't admit your plans to murder millions, yellow...

You still can't tell people how much is owed for the state pensions by the state.

Well, 5,300 bn pounds.

Taxation at 550 bn, spending at 700 bn can't pay for that.

So the states not going to be able to pay.

That's the reality, running a ponzi is going to push people into poverty.

Now the one bit of truth in your statement, is that pension debts in the UK are lower than in Europe. Given that the UK is bust, and they have higher debts and no assets too, what can you conclude from that?

It's going to go bust in Europe first.

France is going south fast, and they have large pension

commitments. Greece has gone already. They couldn't pay, so they have been slashing like mad. The latest wizz is cuts, but back dated. So you don't get any payments until you've paid for the money you had received. Pretty vicious of a state to do that to its citizens Not a banker in sight.

The UK government, of course, lower state pension commitments than the average European country

Ah that argument. Europe is screwed, that must mean the UK is safe. Hmmm. Lets see. Your sister's pregnant, so you can't be pregnant. Balance hey! Or is it that Europe is more pregnant that the UK, or is it more bankrupt than the UK. Can you be a 'little bit pregnant'

The borrowing is paid out of current taxes. Interest and principle.

Pension is paid out of current taxes. Both are liabilities.

You're not asking the right question. That's how big is the liability, and can it be paid out of taxes. For that you need to know the total liabilities of the state. That you can't provide the answer, and deny that it even has to be paid, leads me to believe that either you've stuck your head up your backside on the matter, or you're trying to defraud people. A civil servant reliant on the cash coming in, so are prepared to hide the debts off the books.

Of course I am. How many will you murder so you don't have to pay tax?

I can provide it, have provided it, you dismissed it. You're the one claiming it doesn't need to be paid, politician. Get your head out the public trough and go to jail for your fraud!

Europe's doing better than the UK, so no surprise where YOUR money's going. You're the one screwing around as well as everything else I see.

And you're the one killing the mothers, so...

Incorrect. And that's right, you refuse to pay tax. Your ponzi scam against the British is typical of your foreign scum, raking in billions in corporate welfare.

Europe is and will be fine. France is far better off than the UK. And you completely mischaracterise the changes in France, of course, which are far less radical than the changes here where you get to die, slowly. Greece could afford to pay, they just And I see, you want to kill 20 million like your idol. Got it. And of course, your bankers are hidden behind your fattened murderous ass.

11

Can Chess Lift Children's Lives?

Can chess make you brainy? Do you have to be brainy to play chess? Which one, if either of these two commonly held beliefs reflects the truth? Most people probably believe both of them. There are many claims of the benefits of getting children involved in playing chess, it is seen as the go to game for extremely intelligent children.

But let's be honest here, the coolest in the school playground have never viewed chess success as anything other than compensation for not being cool. You either get to be cool, or to be a chess champion, the two can never be compatible. Or so the thinking goes.

To get a real perspective on the interest of children's chess, I canvassed the views of chess coach Richard Weekes, who founded his own Chess Academy in south east London, and runs clubs across the capital. He is a real believer in the power of chess. He says:

"Chess is a great game that's easy to learn and should be taught in a way that is fun. Playing chess helps to improve children's thinking skills and allows them to explore new ideas."

Over the years, a host of films, and stories have brought glamour and relevance to the game that has made people think differently. One of the oldest of these films now is Knights of the South Bronx portraying Ted Danson as a washed-up teacher who is rejuvenated by steering a deprived call of pupils to New York State Chess Championships. Another well-known American chess movie is Searching for Bobby Fischer which features a more traditional chess hero doing battle with a Svengali type figure to go on to win in his own way.

With the rise of technology, you now don't even need to go near a real chess board and many technological versions of the game, such as Chessfire. You can play with an unknown electronic opponent, or an anonymous but real player on the other side of the world, or someone who is completely anonymous.

Weekes believes that when children play chess, it can empower them in their wider lives:

"Playing chess helps to decrease the reaction time of children in certain situations and allows them to think a little longer about choosing more positive options so that they can respond and act more appropriately".

A new chess film due for theatrical release in the UK in autumn 2016, is Queen of Katwe, made by Disney/ESPN is set to draw more attention to the game. It is based on the real-life story of Phiona Mutesi, a Ugandan child chess prodigy. This will bring renewed interest in girls chess playing, so how appealing is chess to girls? Weekes comments:

One slight disappointment I have though is the noticeable absence of young girls and teenage girls who do not yet play chess. I have been promoting and raising awareness about this for a few years to encourage participation as I believe girls can play chess equally as well as boys. I'd like to think that more girls coming into chess is not that far away though, and what I think could help change this is to have more visible images of chess so that people can see these images around their neighbourhood. For more information, contact Richard Weekes's Chess Academy.

Richard Weekes, Founder of the Richard Weekes Chess Academy

12

Closer Engagement Between Women's Rights and Disability Rights Is a Key Theme for International Women's Day 2015

Where does a disabled woman go for rights advice and support? Many might say if her needs are about access or disability health rights, she should go to a disability rights organisation. If her rights issue is about sexism or sex discrimination she should seek help and support from a women's rights organisation. But why should she have to choose? Rights issues are often complex, dynamic and if a woman is also disabled (or indeed have any other personal characteristic deemed minority such as gender status, race or sexual orientation) she often finds it difficult to navigate to the correct support network.

The mainstream woman's movement has frequently been accused of looking at female empowerment and equality through a fairly rosy lens. High profile feminist activists have historically been from very educated backgrounds, and sometimes taken an academic stance to women's equality. Gay women, trans women, poor women, and black women have historically found their problems sometimes marginalised by the feminist agenda. Feminist preoccupation with campaigns such as equal pay, right to work, equality in housework, and female representation on Boards are all valid subjects of focus for the women's agenda, but many women face adversities that prevent them from even being in a position to confront such problems.

"We have heard from disabled women who were rejected by mainstream women's organisations because of the prejudice and poor status associated with disability. But there are also examples where disabled women were welcomed with open arms and even held highly responsible positions within the women's organization"

These challenges faced by women in the West are hugely magnified by disabled women in poor countries. Andrae, with her colleague Sylvie Cordier from the Gender and Development

Network, will be addressing this subject at this year's African Initiatives Annual Women's Rights Conference, which marks International Women's Day each year. Their workshop will focus on the life conditions of women and girls with disabilities in developing countries and how to ensure they get included in the development process.

In moving forward it is important that both disability rights organisations and women's rights organisations seek a collaborative approach. Karen Andrae notes:

"There is a journey for both but it is mainly about understanding each other's situation, i.e. to understand the issues they have in common and the specific issues of disabled women. There are definite parallels to be drawn between discrimination lived by women and discrimination lived by disabled people, all linked to negative attitudes and prejudices".

In seeking to develop joint and collaborative approaches, there is a concern that disability and women's rights organisations may need to choose to discard their priorities, or dilute their focus to achieve greater inclusion. But this needs not be the case argues Andrae:

"Feminist activist need to realise that they are missing a huge opportunity in gaining additional voices to raise pressure and to really represent all women. Disabled women need to become more pro-active in recognising common concerns beyond disability issues without having to abandon those. There are many examples of really good practice and those need to be shared more to encourage disability right activists and feminist activists to close ranks more consistently".

With UK political attention firmly focused on the 2015 general election, Andrae points out that the year is important for global focus on action for disabled women:

"2015 is a crucial year for everyone both in developing but also in developed countries, with the Sustainable Development Goals (SDGs) being discussed and agreed later in the year. Leave no one behind was the message of the UN Secretary General in the report on post-2015 in June 2013. This message has to be adopted by all parties and we need to ensure that development processes do not reach only low hanging fruits as with the MDGs; full and active participation of representatives of all groups including disabled people, and particularly disabled women, is needed in development processes and their monitoring."

The African Initiatives Women's Rights conference is on Saturday 7 March 2015, 9.30am - 4.15pm in Central Bristol. Contact African Initiatives for more information on attending the conference.

13

African Initiatives Annual International Women's Rights Conference 2014

International Women's Day is observed on 8th March every year, to celebrate the achievements of women; to inspire women to achieve, and to mobilise action for injustices against women. An upcoming rights conference is to be held in Bristol, to mark this event, and highlight the work of key campaigners and champions of women's global empowerment.

African Initiatives is a Bristol-based UK rights charity that delivers projects in Tanzania and Ghana, with the key objectives of improving the life chances of women, girls, disabled and marginalised people.

It's projects focus on rights such as education, health, and equal access to a country's resources, and aims to promote empowerment of people in these areas.

Raising awareness of, and promoting global education at home is an important strand of the international development work of the charity, and African Initiatives also runs a schools programme, and has strong links with local universities and educational institutions.

Central to its global education programme is the annual International Women's Rights Conference, to mark International Women's Day, which will take place on Saturday 1st March this year in central Bristol. The guest speaker is Maanda Ngoitiko, one of the partners of African Initiatives from Tanzania. Maanda is a Maasai woman, and founder and director of the Pastoral Women's Council, a woman-led charity working with women and girls in northern Tanzania.

The conference will also hear from inspirational speakers on acid violence, forced marriage, sex work, colonialism and same-sex relationships, and the experience of women working in hazardous Asian garment factories.

Interest by British people in contributing to international aid has remained strong in terms of charitable donations at times of disaster; but how strong is the commitment to doing more?

The British Government has recently announced that it will reverse its earlier decision, and now allow several hundred of the most vulnerable Syrian refugees to come to Britain. A recent YouGov Poll published on 23 January 2014 posed the question:

"Some European countries are agreeing to each admit a few hundred of the people in the Syrian refugee camps. Do you think the United Kingdom should or should not also agree to admit a few hundred refugees from Syria to settle here?"

The results showed that most British people are against the plans with only 39% saying that we should accept Syrian refugees. Of the remainder, 47% said we should not accept them, and 14% indicating they did not know.

Asked to comment on British public attitudes towards international development, chief executive of African Initiatives, José Sluijs-Doyle, feels there is support, and comments:

"Recent research has found that the UK public is less supportive when it comes to increasing the level of UK aid at a time of economic hardship; however global development is generally viewed as a positive. There is a great interest in understanding how and why development works, and how individuals in developing countries can participate in this process. This interest in global development is further reflected in the increasing number of participants who attend our annual Women's Rights Conference, as well as the high number of volunteers who support us in our work."

The conference will be opened by George Ferguson, Mayor of Bristol, and is open to anyone with an interest in hearing about achievements and campaigns in global women's rights and empowerment. The Annual International Women's Right's Conference by African Initiatives is on Saturday 01 March 2014. Book a place here.

14

Khalsa Aid's Humanitarian Relief in Somerset Shows a Glimpse of a Future Post-Racial Britain

Whilst the British Government has been immobilised by indecision, and confusion about its strategic response to the winter floods, Somerset has been left to drown. Large parts of the UK have been submerged under flood waters for months. No. 10 has failed to act as people in the region watch helplessly as their homes, businesses, cattle and crop become subsumed by contaminated water.

Amid the belated Prime Ministerial visits, a royal visit, apologies, blaming, tears and recriminations, the actions of a Slough based charity stands out with its simple, clear effort. Khalsa Aid, a Sikh charity was set up in 1999 to mark the 300th anniversary of the birth of the movement. In recognition of the achievements of the movement in the UK, and observing the plentiful fare on offer at his Khalsa Centre, that Ravi Singh was motivated to launch the charity's first humanitarian effort in Kosovo.

Recent missions by Khalsa Aid in the Philippines and Haiti have now been followed by a new operation in Somerset last weekend. Observing the failure of authorities to take effective action, and noting that had this flooding taken place in a impoverished country, Khalsa Aid, and other disaster relief charities would have taken action.

This recognition led Khalsa Aid founder, Ravi Singh, to link with a partner in Somerset, and travel to the region to provide manpower, and emergency supplies, which has been welcomed in the area. The television images of Sikhs forming part of a line, side by side with local community volunteers, to pass along supplies, is inspiring, but should not be remarkable.

As Singh says, this is his country and he is simply contributing as a fellow countryman. Sikh faith observers are visibly different from the local inhabitants of the West Country with the rich difference of their appearance, but are not strangers to the area, for Singh confessed that like many in the UK, he goes to the Somerset for his holidays.

A post-racial utopia, in Britain, is one where racial and religious difference does not define the rules of engagement. It is a word where anyone can comfortably live anywhere, a world without ghettos based on race, colour, religion and language. Anyone can go into any shop, barber, hair salon, and expect a service from whoever is working there. No one should have to shop for ordinary services at specialist areas. We should all know each other well enough to live comfortably side by side, irrespective of difference.

We are supposed to be in a post-racial Britain at this point in time. Equality legislation and its protections for ethnic minorities are being eroded. All forms of hate crime, particularly religious hate crime, is on the increase, showing we still have a long journey ahead.

As a faith-based, ethnic minority charity, the action of Khalsa Aid in Somerset provides a glimpse of what a post-racial Britain could look like. True, like politics, disaster makes strange bedfellows. When the flood waters have subsided, the houses dried out, and businesses back up on their feet, this is the side by side integration, and understanding that must become part of race relations in British future. A future where racial and religious differences are not causes for division, suspicion and discrimination, but for celebration. Difference can be cohesive, and Khalsa Aid has shown us how.

15

Acculturation or Diversity: Have the Questions Raised in Felix Dexter's Comedy Been Answered?

The death of acclaimed British actor, comedian and writer Felix Dexter last week, triggered moving tributes in the press and on social media. A stunning performer of stage, theatre, and television, his big break came with the BBC television classic 1990's show The Real McCoy. He went on to perform in the Fast Show, Absolutely Fabulous, with the Royal Shakespeare Company, and more recently in Citizen Khan, currently running on BBC television. He was also hugely successful on the live show circuit where he reproduced his creations to uproarious applause.

Dexter was an acute observer of race dynamics in the UK, and used this to produce brilliant comedy performances. His character Nathaniel, the Nigerian part- time cab driver and part time accountancy student was a great exemplar of this. Nathaniel dressed in white shoes, over stylised suits, and snootily criticised 'West Indians' to whom he felt superior because of their lesser commitment to the British way of life. Dexter's characterisation of Nathaniel spoke to many of the truths of life in the UK at the time: the struggles of African and Caribbean, and other migrants, to understand what it meant to be British, and how to dress in order to demonstrate assimilation. Dexter was a 'West Indian', playing a ridiculous African, who ridiculed 'West Indians' was genius.

It was important to fit in and showed you belonged as differences would be beaten out of you by a rampaging bovver boot. Nathaniel's, ludicrously inappropriate formal dress, gave a message of aspiration that many black and Asian migrants held at the time. Many were from middle class backgrounds in their country of origin, but found themselves driving buses, sweeping the streets, driving cabs, portering or working as low graded nurses. Although these jobs paid the bills, they were meant to be temporary until they could qualify as accountants, lawyers and doctors. But discrimination, inequality and the low paid jobs, with long anti social hours meant part time study programmes extended indefinitely. And for many, those accountancy or law exams were never taken.

Similarly, his other very popular character creation was Douglas, the 'Roots and Culture' lawyer, the embodiment of erudite upper class sophistication, with frequent 'break outs' of patois. The depiction of Douglas's confusion was not about culture clash but about posing the big question of when black migrants would be allowed to be truly English, by their own and other's definition. Is it acceptable for successful black people to have white partners, live in rural areas, enjoy affluent lifestyles beyond limits that were sometimes self-imposed? Can one remain authentic and true to one's cultural heritage, language, dialect and achieve the dizzying heights of life in Cobham as Douglas has? How do black people negotiate the myriad of lifestyle choices with the white Britain, each other, and the family back home? And what of the expectations of the host nation? Did assimilation truly mean equal competition for a share of all the resources the UK had to offer, or only those that were not wanted by the host population? These questions continue to produce tensions today and few can comfortably answer them.

People of African and Caribbean heritage shared together in this discrimination, and Dexter's Nathaniel was one of the few opportunities people had to openly confront how they were turning against each other, and how ridiculous it was. It was unifying to laugh together at Nathaniel and Douglas.

Those who had the pleasure to know and work with Dexter, attest his goodness, talent and humility through the medium of social media. For the rest of us, he appeared to be all that and his untimely death, has robbed us an unbounded talent, still in his prime.

16

Improved Aspirations of Black Pupils Should Be Commended Not Condemned

The Universities Central Council on Admissions (UCAS) has this week published new research on the demand for places at British Universities. UCAS is the organisation responsible for managing applications to universities in the UK. The findings for 2013 showed that there has been a 70% increase in the number of English black pupils applying for a place at a British university since 2006. In 2006, only 20% of black pupils applied to university and this has now risen to 34% and is the largest increase of any ethnic group during this period. English pupils from Chinese and Asian backgrounds have consistently had the highest rates of all pupils seeking university places, and this trend has continued. English pupils from a white ethnic background are now least likely of all ethnic groups to seek a university place and this is a trend seen since 2009.

The increased aspirations of black pupils are to be applauded as higher education is more likely to lead to successful careers and higher income. Well educated citizens with improved employment prospects, irrespective of ethnic background are highly desirable for the economic development and social stability of any nation. For ethnic minorities, who in the UK are more likely to experience a range of social, health, and educational inequalities, this is good news.

However, this success has been tinged by an emerging rhetoric which views this as bad news, and as threatening to the social stability of the country. Advancement in one ethnic group does not mean reduced opportunities for another. It is now two years since the introduction of increased university fees, and although this research suggests that pupils from disadvantaged backgrounds are applying for places in higher numbers than ever, further research must be conducted into why white British pupils are applying for university places. The other significant factor is the stagnation of the British economy during this period. What has been the impact on fears of white teenagers and families about repaying university fees? Are there differences in awareness and knowledge of the loan system in white teenagers compared with ethnic minorities?

There is already an ugly narrative entering mainstream British political and social debate, worsening since 2010, that 'outsiders' are taking away the NHS, school places, housing and jobs from 'indigenous' British people. Accusations that 'politically correct' policies exist in state schools to direct resources towards ethnic minority pupils, and disabled pupils at the expense of white pupils is another unsubstantiated claim that has been in circulation. It is important that higher education does not become part of this discourse and that achievement by all pupils can be acknowledged and unconditionally praised.

17

Can members of the Armed Forces live side by side with communities?

The tragic murder of British soldier Lee Rigby in London exposed the sometimes-uneasy juxtaposition of the military and civil society. At some point, the attackers would have familiarized themselves with the day to day movements, and patterns of army life of the soldiers and families of the Woolwich army barracks. Drummer Rigby was a familiar figure at the local kebab shop, and felt comfortable enough to declare his status as a soldier, or at least someone who was an army sympathizer by wearing a 'Help for Heroes' shirt

Civilians choose to be oblivious of the realities of the work of soldiers in the field. Returning military personnel who experience the theatre of war know the value of what they do when on tours. On return, however, such is the nature of their work they cannot talk about their achievements to their families or civilian friends who feel squeamish about what soldiers have been doing abroad. A recent example of this is when Prince Harry was heavily criticised for his comments on return from Afghanistan when he was bluntly admitted to killing of insurgents. There were fears of a backlash against him personally, but also concern that he should not have been so graphic in talking about what he was doing. For Harry, it would have been completely normal to speak in this way in Afghanistan, with other soldiers. But all people want to know or hear about from returning military is that they have been 'brave' and 'glorious'. No details about killing, as that is outside the experience of most people who if we think too deeply about this, start to feel uncomfortable about the killer in our midst. Killing for a job is not nice. It is not something a father or mother can talk proudly to their children about, as a teacher can at the end of a day's work.

So there has always been a sense of the armed forces doing something different that set their experience apart from that of their civilian neighbours. Integration back to ordinary life has always been difficult for military personnel, and society has not always understood their needs. A research report published in 2012 by the Kings Centre for Military Research found that 13 per cent of returning personnel committed an act of violence in the first few weeks after their return.

Evidence on public attitudes to the armed forces suggests a high level of public respect and acceptance, even though their missions in Iraq and Afghanistan do not have high levels of public support. Does this mean that the armed forces can in general, expect to live in harmony alongside communities? Probably. Incidents such as happened in Woolwich, London is unprecedented and resulted in worldwide headlines and shock, indicating how extremely rare it is.

The Future Reserves 2020 programme will see a significant increase in the use of military reservists will be relied upon in greater numbers following cuts in Ministry of Defence. People in ordinary jobs will be working as army, naval, air, and royal marine reservists in their spare time. This could contribute to strengthening support for participation in military life from ordinary citizens. It could also strengthen the bond between military and the citizen.

National rituals and ceremonies have been developed to engender pride, recognition, and gratitude. These include the parliamentary tribute at the start of Prime Minister's Questions after the death of a soldier, repatriation ceremonies for the deceased, and parades of returning soldiers. On 29 June British personnel will celebrate their military roles with the annual 'Uniform To Work Day' and go to their usual places of work donning their military uniforms to engender community pride and raise awareness of how people are delivering military roles alongside ordinary jobs.

While it is to be anticipated that Woolwich will heal in time, some suspicions will never be overcome, and some the political will always be personal.

Blogs on Arts and Reviews

18

Elizabeth Anionwu's Memoir: Mixed Blessings From a Cambridge Union Exceeds All Superlatives

Elizabeth Anionwu is a diminutive woman of colossal talent in everything she has turned her hand to, and to top off a high achieving career, her memoir has now outed her as a wonderful author. She was born in 1947, from the relationship between her father, a Nigerian student, and her mother Mary, a Classics student whose family came from County Wexford and County Down, in Ireland, to settle in Liverpool. Their romance blossomed at Cambridge University, at a time of discrimination against both black and Irish people in England.

Born into a strong Catholic family on her mother's side, Elizabeth's arrival, to unmarried parents, was a shock to her mother's family threatening to bring great shame to the family.

Elizabeth's mother made the brave decision to keep her baby daughter, against a background of stigmatisation of illegitimate children. The plan was for the baby to be brought up by Mary's parents as their own, but Mary left out one fact that the child would be mixed race, which rapidly jettisoned that plan.

Baby Elizabeth was then brought up in the care of Catholic nuns until she was reunited with her parents, and Irish family, aged nine. The storyline of how she tracked down and met her father is as riveting as the tone of the whole book.

The book charts the fascinating story of her journey through a great number of childhood adversities, including severe beatings at the hands of her stepfather, racism and exclusion, and how she overcame it to become a nurse, health visitor, educator and PhD, and Emeritus Professor of Nursing at the University of West London. She was awarded the CBE in 2001.

A great campaigner, Elizabeth's own adversities in childhood drove her to champion the underdog, and for social justice whether for her patients, or for a better deal for colleagues, particularly nurses. She was an early champion of better care and treatment for those affected by Sickle Cell Disease in the UK. I have met Elizabeth several times at conferences and health events and have heard her speak with great enthusiasm, vigour and passion for her causes, which are always about other people. It was wonderful that she joined the campaign for a statute of Jamaican nurse Mary Seacole, heroine of the Crimea, to be built at St Thomas's hospital, London, against vocal opposition from those who did not want to see a black nurse elevated and celebrated in this way.

This memoir is emotional, startling, astonishing, wondrous and funny. We feel great emotion for what Elizabeth had to endure as a child, and feel emotional for her parents, particularly her mother who bore a great personal toll for because of pregnancy. The reader is startled and astonished to observe Elizabeth immerse herself in all the positive joys of life, despite her childhood, and feel a sense of wonder as she achieves one fantastic accomplishment after another. Finally, we laugh with her as she applies a dry humour to and sense of fun to the many situations she found herself in.

We are treated, unexpectedly, to a social history of childcare, housing, social care and health particularly public health, in an extremely informative and personal way.

The expression 'reading for pleasure' will resonate as highly truthful with Professor Anionwu's fantastic memoir.

Elizabeth Anionwu's memoirs 'Mixed Blessings from a Cambridge Union' are available in paperback at £14.99 (ISBN: 978-0-9955268-0-8) online from Amazon & Waterstones & can be ordered from bookstores. They can also be downloaded as an e-book (£6.99) from Kindle Amazon & Kobo. Please visit her website for more information: http://www.elizabethanionwu. co.uk Visit Elizabeth's Facebook Page: https://www.facebook. com/SickleToSeacoleMemoirs/

Emeritus Professor Elizabeth Anionwu; *Photograph by Barney Newman*

Author Elizabeth Anionwu, aged 9 months being visited by her mother, in a Catholic care home in 1948 in Birmingham. *Copyright Elizabeth Anionwu*

19

An Evocative and Positive New Album by The Stone Foundation: A Life Unlimited

The Stone Foundation is a band driven by an unrelenting passion for a gorgeous fusion of original jazz/soul/funk music, which they continue to share with their latest album release, A Life Unlimited. The brainchild of Neil Jones (lead vocal) and Neil Sheasby (bass), the band is now a deliciously cohesive meld of soul/jazz/funk and rock musicians. A solid, retro and contemporary horn section is provided by Gareth John (trumpet), Gary Rollins (sax) and Adam Stevens on baritone sax. The album was written by Jones/Sheasby, with John contributing to the penning of Old Partners, New Dances.

The album title will need little explanation for the band's strong fan base who will know that the album is all about making your own luck, taking charge of life, transforming setbacks into opportunities, and doing what it takes to live the life of your dreams. The backdrop for the band is of a highway of musicians such as The Specials, Weller, The Selecter, The Beat, soul sounds, and British Brit rock-pop. The band has a dedication to loving and sharing all of the shades of this heritage, without a 'use by' date normally attached to contemporary music.

The Stone Foundation: Photograph by Lee Cogswell

This is a band that has made things happen for themselves, with a dollop of good luck, and a lot of hard work to make that luck happen. They capture this in the brilliant track, A Love Uprising, featuring Dr Robert Howard Blow Monkeys frontman, funnelling the message of the album title, and sentiment behind the band's journey and philosophy. The lyrics sound out :"The world seems clearer in natural light/ there's no progression without a fight/ don't try to tell me that you've got no choice/ first step to freedom starts with a solitary voice" and " When you gonna start to realise that you are somebody/keep climbing til you reach the top for a life unlimited/ keep running don't ever stop, take the initiative/just keep shining the light of love, don't ever stop it's what you are, no show me your love uprising."

This positivity and determination has taken the band to deals with labels in Japan and the USA. Jones told me how the Japanese deal came about:

"A guy who works for visit Britain in Japan wanted to showcase a band that sold out venues in London and show the Japanese public a taste of English music. He was a big fan of the band and after a quick introduction from a friend of ours in London the rest is history. We had an element of luck but have really grabbed the opportunity with both hands and after a lot of hard work and three amazing tours in Japan we head out to play Fuji Rock (Japan's biggest festival) in a couple of weeks, with a record deal for A Life Unlimited in Japan with P Vine records in Tokyo. We've had some amazing times so far in Japan and long may it continue, we feel really blessed"

My favourite track on the album is undoubtedly Old Partners, New Dances, which is an incredibly evocative jazz instrumental. This is the kind of track that makes you selfish. You are in a music club, and this comes on, and you definitely want everyone around you to stop talking, and the room to recede so the music and come forward into your space so it is just you and it. Think smoky, languid, whisky and gin, piano, sax and a selfish hedonism in the corner of the club.

Diversity is a key word for this album, and the tracks all tell different stories of striving, empowerment, fulfillment and achievement. Speak Your Piece is a wonderfully visioned, crafted and delivered with Jones' delivery of an alternately pained and passionate, motivational vocal. Jones says about this track:

"Lyrically its 2 songs coming together to make one, the main section was written by myself and the last section was put together by Neil Sheasby. The feel really came from Phil, Sheasby and Ian. I was inspired by listening to tracks from albums by Sly Johnson and Marvin Gaye and really wanted to write something that had a social commentary. Every time I turn the TV on lately the world seems to be spiraling into an uncontrollable mess, war hungry politicians, corrupt governments, greedy bankers etc. etc. The song for me is kind of a reminder to love the people close to you, to take time to be thankful for what you have and in the process hopefully spread a little positivity. Positivity really is an infectious thing, that's kind of the idea behind the album title."

The band has attracted several similarly rhythm-loving artists and features contributions from Graham Parker (The Night Teller), US soul stalwart Nolan Porter (Beverley), vocal harmony group The Four Perfections (Pushing Your Love) and Blow Monkeys front man Doctor Robert Howard (A Love Uprising).

There has been fantastic pre-release support for the album, doing well in the pre-order charts, and the band appreciates everything that has come their way, and they have made happen. Neil Jones told me how the band is feeling about where it's at right now:

"It really is an extremely exciting time for us, we've just signed record deals in Japan with P Vine and in America with Spectra and with each year the band seems to step up and get stronger and stronger. We never make the same record twice and we're always trying to mix things up. We've had personnel changes along the way as well, which has really helped freshen things up, a lot of the time we have to shake things up because people lack the vision to see the new ideas through, so we just get new players in. Every record we make always feels like the first to me, we're always striving for better, it's a deeply personal experience making a n Stone Foundation record. The fans and followers of the band mean a lot to us too, we are really lucky to have such a loyal fan base and one that keeps on growing every year we play".

A Life Unlimited, is released in the UK on 7 August. Find out more about the band and pre-order the album here: http://www.stonefoundation.co.uk/

The Stone Foundation: Photograph by Lee Cogswell

The Stone Foundation: Photograph by Lee Cogswell

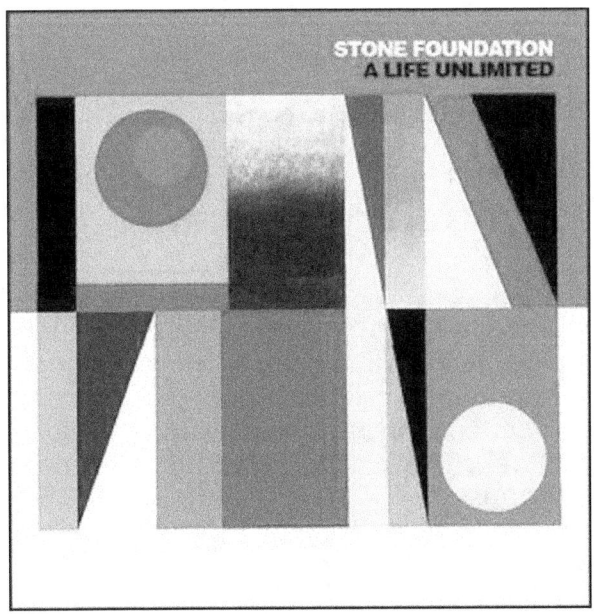

A Life Unlimited by the Stone Foundation

20

Remember The Skanking TV Pigeon? The Selecter's New Album 'Subculture' Is The Soundtrack Of Summer 2015

Subculture is the rhythm-packed, vibrant, fresh new album from The Selecter, and listening to it you understand why this band has remained relevant, and with a strong following today. The album is a 12-track work and is mostly co-penned by Pauline Black, the iconic voice of contemporary ska/reggae/2-tone music.

Arthur 'Gaps' Hendrickson, also co-writer on several of the album tracks, is the only other original member of the band, and though the band is not overly focused on nostalgic backward glancing, it is somewhat charming to know that these two are still a combined force. Gaps's authentic and credible MC'ing and harmonic vocalizations are a pleasure to listen to as this is a voice you have to search hard to hear today. With new members, I wanted to know whether it sometimes felt like two bands, a mix of the old and the new. The band said:

'The Selecter is a constantly evolving band bringing together former members and the best new crop of talent we can find. Bands have to refresh occasionally - at the moment just like our new single says, we are 'Boxfresh'.

This is a band that has always had appeal for those on the fringes of society, the subcultures, the Mods, the Rockers, the Rude Boys and Rude Girls, Ska, Reggae, and Punk followers. It is a pull for those that love the street as a place to meet, chat, laugh, and listen to music.

The first track is 'Box Fresh', a passionate, soulful ska-based rhythm, setting out a commitment to the here and now, and always keeping things alive, wanting to know the new and emerging. Black's searing lead vocal promises 'a box fresh start, a brand new beginning'. She demands though, that change and freshness is good, but we must make sure we 'make it rude'. To keep things fresh, many bands with the longevity of the Selecter are often asked about which current acts they would be interested in working with. The band has clear ideas:

'Janelle Monae & Bruno Mars spring to mind- after all they are half way there with their fashion sense. Perhaps Mark Ronson would like to produce!'

A lover's rock and dancehall vibe makes an appearance on the track 'It never worked out', and you can imagine it playing at a party at the end of the night, when energy is flagging, and one final track is put on that invigorates the party again - this is the one.

For activists, justice and rights campaigners, 'Breakdown', set against a reggae dub and bass, and reverberating vocals, is the stand out track. This is about police brutality, injustice and misuse of lethal force by the police. The song's tragic roll call of people killed by the system, whether that system is race-based street thuggery, institutional restraint procedures, police shootings, or people innocently caught in the cross-fire of gang related shootings. Stephen Lawrence, Cherry Groce, Joy Gardner, Charlene Ellis and Letitia Shakespeare, Roger Sylvester, Trayvon Martin, Michael Brown and Mark Duggan are all name checked, sadly for the manner of their deaths. 'Somethings are so wrong, nothing ever makes it right. There's gonna be a breakdown, a social breakdown, we've heard it all before' sings Black. This is my personal track of choice on the album.

A cover version of Patti Smith's 'Because the Night', co-penned by Smith and Bruce Springsteen appears on the album. The ska treatment, with Gaps toasting over Black's strong delivery of the melody really brings an interesting dynamic to this track and updates it.

There is a resurgence of interest in ska, reggae and 2- tone, with it featuring as the back drop to a number of television adverts, one featuring 'On my radio' all bringing in a new audience, and reeling back in the old audience who perhaps life has led away from ska. Selecter fans recently did a double take on hearing 'On my radio' , featuring a dancing pigeon as the back drop to a banking advertisement, and although it happened as a publishing deal rather than something the band actioned, they have taken it in good humour:

'Everybody in The Selecter thought that a pigeon dancing to 'On My Radio' for nearly a minute on TV was the coolest thing ever! That bird knew how to skank too!'

The immediate future is very busy for the band with many live performances ahead:

'We have festival performances throughout this summer, and an extensive headline UK tour booked in for November so that's as far as we know about for now. However, Australia & North & South America beckon in 2015, and there will be UK dates too'.

Yes, 1979 through 1981 were electrifying years for The Selecter, but 2015, with Subculture, they are stronger than ever. This album must be recommended as one of the sound tracks of summer 2015.

Subculture is out June 15. Visit http://www.theselecter.net/

Pauline Black and 'Gaps' The Selecter: (Photo: The Selecter)

The Selecter: Subculture (Photo:The Selecter)

21

Author Alex Wheatle's New Novel Can Inspire Young Black Males Away from Gang Violence

In June 2006 I was working in youth health services on Black Prince Road, Lambeth in London when a 15 year old black boy was stabbed to death by a gang of around 10 others. When I arrived for work the morning after, the street was still littered with scattered debris, the remnants of the previous night's fierce and deadly battle, and after the police had removed their evidence. The dead boy was known among friends as 'Tiny Alien' due to his diminutive stature, and cute features. His parents were incredulous that this could happen to their good, studious son, real name Alex Mulumba, who had ambitions of becoming an engineer. Alex's bereft father denied his son's involvement with gangs or weapons but it was to be after his death that his father learned of the full extent of his son's membership of a well-known, notorious local gang, and that he was killed by members of a rival gang.

Painful evidence of this soon emerged with pictures of Alex Mulumba posing on a website holding gangster weapons. This was to prove to be a familiar pattern with the gang-related murders of 'good' black boys who were subsequently found to be heavily involved in youth gang life, in other words, they were 'bad' all along. The harm to the black community is compounded by the realities that the perpetrators are often young black males. Mulumba's killer was Abu Sarpong, aged 18 years given a life sentence, with a minimum 14 year tariff. The cause of the killing was a minor altercation earlier in the day.

The search for answers has focused on the black family and black communities, and there are certainly questions to be asked there. Is it to do with fatherless families without strong male role models that creates a vacuum to be filled by a Mr Big?

This is one factor explored in the new Young Adult fiction book by Alex Wheatle, 'Liccle Bit' dramatises a toxic set of circumstances that sees 'good boy' Lemar (nicknamed 'Liccle Bit' due to his small stature) drawn fairly easily into life as a young gangster.

'Liccle Bit' is Wheatle's first work for the Young Adult sector, but his own background as a black male who grew and developed against a backdrop of inner - city deprivation, has given him much to draw on. The novel is a triumph in observational writing, accurately capturing the rhythms and flavours of Black British life. The dialogue is witty, fast and very funny, adding to the tragedy of the action that sees Lemar drawn from being a 'good boy', to one who gets in deep with gang life. A talented young artist from a loving family with all the modern day challenges, he involves himself in activities that threaten to bring catastrophe to the door of his family.

Wheatle is also very close to his subject through the youth work he does, and through visiting schools, prisons and Youth Offending Institutions where he has got close up to the issues. A book like 'Liccle Bit' is a great read, and if it can be read by young black males it could have a positive impact. Who did Wheatle have in mind when writing the book? He said:

"Liccle Bit is for everybody to enjoy and learn from and if it engages those students from all sort of backgrounds where reading is not the top off their priorities then that's a bonus. From my experiences of visiting schools, literacy levels are going down so if I can encourage any student to pick up a book and engage in a good tale then that's brilliant".

In this general election year, politicians are in listening mode, so what message would Wheatle wish to transmit to them? Inequalities and confused messages about literacy would be at the top of the list:

"I would make it compulsory for every school to have a library. We have to give all our children every chance of progression and social mobility. Every student has to be given hope that their time in education is for a purpose and will be rewarded. The foundation of that is to have excellent comprehension and reading skills. With the aforementioned, they can study and research any subject with confidence. That is why I would suggest that I would include in the school curriculum a half hour of every week to be dedicated for reading for pleasure."

Alex Wheatle was awarded the MBE for services to literature in 2008, after an acclaimed literary career starting with Brixton Rock, his first novel, which was followed by a further six novels.

Liccle Bit will be published by Atom Books on 5 March 2015

Alex Wheatle: Author of Liccle Bit

22

Zombie XI by Peter Kalu

I have the pleasure of reviewing Zombie XI, the new Children and Young Adult novel by award winning author Peter Kalu, to be published by Hope Road on 4 August 2016

The overarching theme is football, and its prominence in the life of Leonard, a rather quirky boy living an upside down life with his mother, but for whom it is easy to make all that seem normal. What is less than normal is the ghostly appearance of the England world cup winning team of 1966:

One by one the players come forward and stand on the touchline right in front of me. Men with skin that peels and reforms, solid yet ghost-like. I look down at my book and then up at them. It is the England 1966 World Cup Final Team. Every one of them.

He now has a team to play with regularly, and they don't respect time or place:

I go to bed and read my football book. I can hear the zzzz zzzz of Carla's sewing machine. It makes me think of how the footballers must have run when the ground had frost on it. Brushing through the frozen grass leaves. Zzz z zzzz. I hear my radiator ticking as it cools. And a very faint shouting from beyond my window. It's a football match. Who would play a match at this hour? The zombies.

Zombie XI's main themes are the 1966 World Cup win anniversary, belonging, rejection, family, racism, cultural diversity. And zombies.

The book is for boys, girls, parents, teachers and anyone who loves a good read. Kalu's fresh, pacy, authentic, funny and poignant dialogue is a joy to read.

Find out more at Peter's website: www.peterkalu.com

Peter Kalu: Author of Xombie X1

BLOGS ON POLITICS AND SOCIAL COMMENTARY

23

Anti-racism work is being undermined by football's leaders

The many achievements of the Kick It Out campaign risk being undermined by the game's leaders. With England taking part in their first World Cup game yesterday, it is timely to look at progress on racism in football. The Kick It Out campaign to end all forms of discrimination in football, and to promote inclusion and diversity, is 21 years old this year, so what has been achieved?

Black players still face abuse on the pitch, and the debate as to what action should follow is undecided. Should the player ignore the abuse? Walk off the pitch? Should the team walk off the pitch? Who should take the lead, politicians, or football's governing bodies?

There is still no definitive position on this, but when Kevin Prince Boateng walked off the pitch following racist chanting during a game he was both criticised and commended for his action.

Failure of black players and managers to progress in football is being addressed by Kick It Out with the launch of its mentoring and leadership programme, aimed at increasing representation and inclusion. The campaign also has a clear Equality Standard which gives best practice guidance for football organisations about employment practices, approaches to dealing with stadium abuse, keeping records of abusive incidents and promoting equality.

In recent years there has been a massive surge in the use of social media as a channel for abuse, which is also being challenged by the work of True Vision, which provides a facility for victims to report online abuse.

The many achievements of the Kick It Out campaign over the years has seen much greater awareness of the issue of discrimination and equality in football, however its work is being undermined by the game's leaders, especially at international level.

Fifa President Sepp Blatter has delivered several confused messages on racism in football, from outright denial that it exists to saying that on pitch handshakes could manage the problem. More recently he claimed that racism underpins the recent allegations of corruption claims against Fifa in the selection of Qatar for the 2022 tournament.

Whilst Blatter's analysis is easily dismissed by informed observers and commentators, ordinary fans may be left trying to make sense of the confusion.

We all know that racism does not begin in concentration camps but as a kernel in the minds of ordinary people, who often are not able to predict the end point of their fledgling discontent. So it is desirable for people to possess a shared understanding of racism, and how to defeat it.

Racism has always been an ugly, uncomfortable concept. When applied to historically or geographically distant inhumane acts, most people easily concur that it is reprehensible.

Bring it closer to home, scale it at the level of everyday, however, and it often becomes too personal for comfort. Political debates have allowed discussion on racism to be obfuscated and conflated with narratives about minority-majority rights to influence national and cultural values.

This needs to be broken down so football fans are confident to report racist and discriminatory actions in stadiums and online.

We know that racial prejudice is currently on the increase at societal level, and continues to be prevalent in many national institutions such as the NHS and the police. Sport in general, and football in particular can lead a potent grassroots movement in the fight against discrimination.

And finally, come on England!

Reader comments:

 Players should simply walk off the pitch, and sod what the Clubs say about 'professional' behaviour in continuing to play amidst a barrage of insults. Its a Human Rights issue and a BME players dignity over rides what the greedy Clubs and thicko fans have to say. No player should be subjected to abuse of monkey chants and bananas and racist comments. If the Clubs sue, then the Black Players Association should fight their case in the Courts.

24

Can anyone still trust the police?

As long as the public cannot see justice being properly exercised in the wake of evidence of police misconduct, then trust will need to be earned, rather than assumed.

What connects a murdered black teenager, a vulnerable man unlawfully killed on the streets of London, football supporters killed in a stadium disaster and a Tory chief whip?

Police misconduct has been implicated in all of these examples, and in the case of the investigation into her son's death, Doreen Lawrence has recently issued a blanket statement claiming that you cannot trust the police.

Following the recent publication of the Ellison report, alleging further corruption by the police during the investigation of Stephen Lawrence's murder in 1993, his father Neville Lawrence acknowledged that the family's fight for justice is continuing.

Lack of trust in the police can often be seen as a problem for black people, and dismissed as people having a chip on their shoulders. But those failed by the police include victims of domestic violence who do not trust police to respond to their needs, people in custody with mental health problems such as Sean Rigg, and the victims of homophobic crimes.

From football fans, to those holding the highest office like Andrew Mitchell, everyone is a potential victim of police misconduct. Mitchell's case prompted a universal cry of 'join the club' from the countless stop and search victims, and others who had shared his experience, and far worse, for decades.

No one wants to believe we cannot trust the police, because public confidence and trust in the police is an essential foundation of civil society, justice, and equality.

The importance of this need to believe and trust the police is so strong that even in the face of evidence to the contrary, public trust in the police remains strong.

Recent evidence suggests that the police remain among the most trusted profession, and even in Andrew Mitchell's case, when holes started to appear in the police claims, public belief in their version of events remained largely unchanged.

This may able account for the inexplicable failing by a jury to convict former PC Simon Harwood after an inquest ruled that Ian Tomlinson had been unlawfully killed by Harwood

We do have to trust the police, but are in the uncomfortable position of knowing that we cannot fully do so. For this reason, many people also prefer to believe the 'bad apples' notion of individual culpability rather than institutional failings.

As long as the public cannot see justice being properly exercised in the wake of evidence of police misconduct, then trust will need to be earned, rather than assumed.

Reader comments:

 All my grandparents generation within my family were miners. I was eight when the miners strike happened. I learnt early that the police are a gang of brutal thugs who lie and collude and fake evidence to get whatever they want. The notion that the police are a non political entity to enforce democratic laws is the problem. They are inherently political. The only way to tackle corruption is to accept they are a group that have their own agenda, they go far beyond protecting and serving. Because they are seen purely as enforcers of law, rather than the frontline judges of law and order that they actually are, they are afforded undue respect and privilege. IMHO there's no way we can end the culture of corruption until we have a serious discussion about our culture as a whole. Someone needs to "police the police" or we could rationally accept that no one group should be given absolute authority in any situation.

 We have to. On the whole the police do a good jog, but a difficult job. Not only to they have to contend with criminals and villains but they are required to police dissidents and all the ragtail of anti social behaviour individuals and families that are anti authority. There is regrettably a culture of anti-authority, disrespect, and downright bolshiness in many communities these days. And it doesn't help in keeping communities safe, particularly when they go out of their way in making the job of policing even more difficult than it already is.

 The Lawrence case is only the tip of the iceberg and where the establishment systems in the UK including the police are general corrupt when you undertake in-depth research of what is really going on internally – http://worldinnovation-foundation.blogspot.co.uk/2014/03/lawrence-case-shows-that-justice-and.html

25

Interest in 'Blonde Angel' will ebb away now Maria is found to be a Roma child

At the time of writing, the news story having been the lead 'breaking news' item, has now slipped to the fourth story on BBC television news.

The mother of the child described as the 'blonde angel' found living with a Roma family in Greece has been identified through DNA evidence as a Bulgarian woman.

This news is consistent with the information provided by the Roma couple in Greece, now incarcerated and facing charges of child abduction.

The authorities investigating the case have rapidly turned the focus of their investigation into identifying whether the child was sold by the biological mother, as this would be a basis for charging them.

Police, social services, the media and some members of communities with Roma people have been driven by this hysteria to behave in ways that only reinforce racist stereotypes of Roma child stealing. This hysteria has led to the snatching, followed by the rapid return of two blond Roma children in Dublin to their families after DNA evidence showed they belonged to the families.

The case of Maria in Greece has triggered an ugly discourse consisting of three main elements:

Roma people are all child abducting criminals. They like to abduct 'blonde angels' and turn them into 'dancing bears' for money; that there are hordes of abducted 'blonde angels', taken from wealthy white families by Roma, and this could have been the fate of Madeline McCann.

Ethnic minority families, and poor people, provide undesirable family environments in which to rear children.

Roma people will soon be in the UK in greater numbers from January 2014. British people had better lock up their blonde children as soon as possible.

That the focus is now on securing grounds for criminalising Maria's biological parents – and possibly the foster parents – is disturbing. How plausible is it that poor Roma parents secure significant financial gains through the selling of children to one another? If the Roma foster family in Greece intended to sell Maria on, would the best time not be when she was a baby, not a child of five or six?

It is much more likely that Maria was given up under the circumstances described by both families.

At the time of writing, the news story having been the lead 'breaking news' item, has now slipped to the fourth story on BBC television news.

Reader comments:

 I remember a book by Dahlov Ipcar about the Gypsies and racial hate in America for us Native Americans in the past with the Incoming 1800 to now humans for EVERYWHERE else on the planet may also have something to do with the theft and child keeping for fear of you all being to be GELFED and GWARed into this kind of genocidal land management issue against us as a different history of human development on the planet and land accordances like in 1945 and 1967 be granted for those of us Hussein and his like have been proven to gen-ocidal towards so we have feet to head In an attached in this space and some hope of communications between all of us to survive rather than the Invasion of America that left Native American populations nearly extinct if not on an unalterable course because of the nature of the stolen weapons used to create the old human genocide situation at all. Hussein was not disclosed properly for his actions in America to also allow them to keep their treaty adequately and he is still not accounted for completely for the ramifications of his actions esp. given the walking bioweapons of Jackson and Bono to stoke fires on what is allowed human medical behavior. How dare you all create incendiary behavior by telling people to lock up only the blue eyed blondes-lock up all your children against your own stupity hate and unknown of self and stop the hate development there while you all have a home. We Native Americans aren't here to be sucked dry rebuilding

Eurasia and Africa Again for your problems and wars. Treat the social disease issue of it -keep better separate and practice quarantine and save yourselves. As the first "white appearing "child in a mixed in America not here family that used to be loving towards it's new children like me I find this statement in need of address for it's malice and potential ramification. We had better homes here before this hate came and view it as a genocidal action in intent and feel better awareness warranted and better protection against the political changes in 50 years or so involving our families and communities here a warranted Hague level hope. With the repetitive unsolved theft of my medical and identity papers here inc. DNA spin and military involvement with most family I fear for the levels sunk in front of us too-no bombs needed computer forth -murder change sex and never be found -Too freak not to be Jackson and obsessionism starting things again for more money and forgetting all the rest of humans for the buck.

Odd in American when they give money and new family it's seen as adoption even if there is question involving he parent. Remember the British couple that thought their adoption here i San Diego Ca was legal and the problems with the BLACKS not the Roma. Over here the blacks are practically your best child thieves and think nothing of outdoing alleged Gypsy tactic to do so for drugs power of minds and government and nobody says a word. Hardly any black kids killed here now but boy watch for them because they don't protect the white kids the way everybody over here and been forced to do nd they are lying cheating raping animals here who should not be tolerated anymore than Khartoum. They protect Indian children even less and are torturous on them most and usually with white help. We are not pro mixed human communities by drug and electrical programming here and don't approve of the way we Native Americans are considered your dumping ground for evil humans a good course of nature and peacekeeping. The introduction of heavier Black and White community mixed here is a nightmare-disease spreads way more often, robbery and money gainning dugwars in the home like the recent French listings indicate a unattended problem, residentail and building maintenance and decay are enormous and fincially destituting he Indian and White more than the blacks and this has to stop. The Irish worked harder here then the Blacks and under just as rough of terms esp. at the hands of the Blacks so I have no qualm in saying the race war there is here like a spreading disease that is creating a genocidal level of change for real original property owners namely us undrugged Native Americans and we are due compensation and removal of these issues by their original government to their origins and our home back and in the order in which it was found.

Exactly! Specially coming after the Madeleine McCann's abduction.
But I have to say that the Roma Community are their own worst enemies, and there is very little of value in the 'culture' they are trying to preserve. No effort is made by them to improve their literacy/educational attainment, and employment rates and social mobility. They really cannot blame anybody else. The rest of the world cannot sit idly by and let this kind of nomadic kind of lifestyle continue. They represent a byegone age, not the C21. I would like to see them integrated into society and accept the responsibilities that society expects of its citizens.

Big news splashed everywhere when the dirty Gypsies are accused of abducting blonde children. But when it turns out the child is actually a Gypsy and the parents aren't child traffickers after-all? Nothing. Silence. Look the other way and pretend it didn't happen. I thought this sort of thing ended at the end of World War II when the Allies discovered what was going on in the Concentration Camps. Wow, am I ever naive. These are not fringe groups attacking the Roma — it's governments behind the removal of the children and racial profiling against the Roma. I wish I could say Canada is different, that we represent a bastion of hope in a nasty, racist world, but just this year Jason Kenney, under the tutelage of Ezra Levant, decided to stop accepting Roma refugees from Hungary into our country based on the exact same stereotypes that led to the child removals. Hungary is now under the control of the neo-N@zis and Canada is playing along with it. Who's next, the Jews?

And if they disagree with the overlords — to gas chambers! Don't laugh. This is no joke. This is where we're heading. But some of us will stand up and try to stop it, even if the Fascists put us in jail. Not in my country.

26

Cameron protects Tory advisor Lynton Crosby and sweeps aside need to tell the truth

In this week's big political interview on the Andrew Marr show, David Cameron showed clear contempt for the public by giving patronising responses to questions about the role played by a Tory advisor in government decisions.

In this week's big political interview on the Andrew Marr show, David Cameron showed clear contempt for the public by giving patronising responses to questions about the role played by a Tory advisor in government decisions.

Lynton Crosby is strategist to the Tory party, and questions have been raised about his role in the government's decision to scrap plans to introduce plain packaging on cigarette boxes given his links with the tobacco industry.

There are also concerns about Crosby's advisory activities with a private health care company in relation to the NHS.

However Cameron assiduously side-stepped questions about whether he had discussed the proposed tobacco strategy with Crosby.

Andrew Marr:

"So can I ask you again whether you have actually talked to him (Crosby) about this issue?"

Cameron:

"Well I think it is important this issue of lobbying because, well look, let me be clear he has not intervened in any way, on this or indeed on other issues and the decision, it's very important people know this, we haven't actually changed our policy, I mean, I think there are merits to plain paper packaging for cigarettes, we need more evidence, we need greater legal certainty, we're not going ahead with it right now, but I certainly don't rule it out for the future.

"So the whole thing actually, from start to finish has been something of a media invention. So, he hasn't intervened, it would be wrong for him to intervene in any way, the decision was actually taken by me, sitting up there (points towards building in No. 10) at my kitchen table, let's not move ahead with this now, we don't have enough evidence, there's too much legal uncertainty."

"But let's be clear, this government has been very tough on tobacco, you know we have said we've got to cut down on these vending machines, we've got to stop big shops doing big promotions, we've carried on with the smoking ban, we've put up the price of cigarettes, and if we're too much in hock to the lobbyists as it were, why have we just published a lobbying Bill?"

Marr:

"You have told me absolutely everything except the question that I was asking, which is have you talked to Lynton Crosby about this?"

Cameron:

"I have answered the question; he has not intervened in any single way."

Marr:

"You haven't actually prime minister, but you won't tell me whether you have talked to him about it?"

Cameron:

"I think as I've said, he hasn't intervened in any single way, I think you'll find that is an answer."

Marr:

"Yes, but its not quite an answer to the question I asked."

Cameron:

"But Its all you're getting (laughs)."

Marr:

"There we go."

Cameron's tone is similar to one he probably uses with his children, with a clear undertone of 'now don't be a naughty boy, I've told you what you have to believe, now run off and play, there's a good boy'.

The public, and the electorate deserves better.

Reader comments:

 Time for Cameron to Go cause he has no respect for the people of this Country and I feel he knows he is gone come the General Election in 2015, so he is destroying all he can between now and then, and he will make sure that he make lie after lie after lie as well

 When you have lost all the policy arguments – attack the the campaign strategist. Good plan – I thought labour was shoo-in for 2015 with coalition facing unpopularity for dealing with Labour's mess – but looks like you are worried now.

 If he doesn't have something to hide why doesn't he answer the question? If he hadn't talked to Crosby about it he'd sure-ly have said so already. The fact he refuses to directly deny it is practically an admission that he has talked to Crosby about these things. That matters.

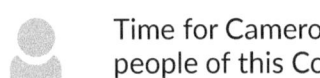 I agree that it shouldn't distract from the larger political issues but this is an issue in its own right. It's about regulato-ry capture at the very highest level. That's a serious issue.

27

The Home Office needs to come clean about taser deaths

Greater Manchester police has referred itself to the Independent Police Complaints Commission (IPCC) following the death of a young man after attending a call out.

Greater Manchester police has referred itself to the Independent Police Complaints Commission (IPCC) following the death of a young man after attending a call out.

Jordan Begley, aged 23, was shot by police with a stun gun this week after police were called to reports of a man armed with a knife. His friends deny that he was armed, and the details of this situation will hopefully come out in the IPCC report.

The Home Office has published routine statistics on the deployment of stun guns in England and Wales since its introduction in England in Wales in 2004, after an initial 12 month pilot.

The deployment figures do not refer to actual use, and Home Office suggests that the weapon is only fired by police in 30 per cent of situations where it is deployed.

This routine referral to the IPCC following each death by British police is an insignificant response, and the lack of published government data on deaths caused by tasers is a human rights issue. The Home Office should now investigate the numbers of deaths following deployment of tasers in England and Wales, the causal factors, and actions taken to review and improve their deployment since they were introduced.

Stun guns are designed to deliver two actions when fired: firstly, it causes rapid muscle immobilisation causing the person to fall; and secondly, it delivers a pain experience, used to quieten the person.

It is intended to be a non-lethal weapon, but there have been many deaths reported following its use in England and Wales, but no research or inquiry has been conducted that takes a high level review of all of the cases.

We currently do not know from published government data the annual pattern of the use of tasers nationally. We do not know how many have died after being shot by tasers since 2003 in England and Wales, and the specific factors contributing to their deaths.

In many cases, the circumstances are contentious with vulnerable victims, and inconclusive inquest results. The demographic background of victims need to be included in this study as a high number appear to come from disadvantaged, poor and vulnerable backgrounds.

What is the picture internationally?

Stun guns are in prolific use internationally, and Amnesty International undertook analysis of stun gun deaths in the United States.

Five hundred deaths since 2001 following the use of tasers in the USA is an exceedingly high rate for a non-lethal weapon. That a human rights organisation conducted this research suggests that US government data on deaths following shooting with stun guns is also the subject of secrecy as it is in the UK.

No one is suggesting that police should not be provided with appropriate technology and equipment to enable a proportionate response to threats, in order to protect themselves and the public.

However, there should be comprehensive and continuous evaluation of the technology, and an inquiry into the potential harms where tasers are used on vulnerable members of the public. Results should be placed in the public domain.

In France there is also concern that police appear to use tasers with impunity.

Again, the responsibility rests with a human rights group, this time, France24, to lead on concerns following significant increases in uses and abuses of the technology (in one cited case, the weapon was discharged by police after someone displayed a 'hostile attitude').

There are concerns in France about the serious injuries and deaths caused by tasers used by police.

Jordan Begley's death should be the one that leads to proper accountability and responsibility for the use of this weapon, and should lead to a comprehensive, independent review of the deaths of those who have died in this callous way after police shootings.

Reader comments:

 I read an article regarding the 10 deaths involved in taser use. Is the writer of this article aware of how the people died? It appears a few shot themselves and died of wounds, a few had stabbed or cut themselves, and one or two may have been on drugs. It is never nice to die, would the writer of this article be happy to go confront a gunman or knife wielding person with a stick and handcuffs??? I thought not, you stay safe behind your desk and criticise everyone else while safely out of harms way. Grow up and get realistic, 10 deaths is a low number... How many people do you think would be dead from these gunmen or knife wielders if they were not stopped?

 This is not an accurate representation to TASER technology. First, we do know the number of deaths in the UK involving a TASER device and there are there have been no causal links between the 5 deaths while 2 further cases are under independent investigation. That's coming clean. Next, you state that Amnesty has cited 500 plus deaths. However, if you read the report, Amnesty is on record stating 60 of the 500+ deaths are cited as causal, contributory or "weren't ruled out" — a far cry from 500+ (read Amnesty's reports) as that doesn't mention that the remaining cases were not caused or contributed by TASER device. How about you come clean AFTER you read the full report in Amnesty's own words? Your closing asks for Jordan Begley's tragic death to lead to accountability, responsibility and a comprehensive, independent review of the deaths of those who have died. We'll gladly take that as will British police any day. But you need to accept the answers. What if something else is the cause of death? Will the cry for blaming TASER devices end their? I doubt it as you clearly won't accept the so called "routine referral to the IPCC" as you call this an insignificant response. How about coming clean in that you are incorrect about saying that since a human rights organisation conducted research suggests that US government data on deaths following shooting with stun guns is also the subject of secrecy as it is in the UK. Secrecy, really? Have you used PubMed to look up all the peer reviewed studies on TASER technology? Have you looked at the studies by the Home Office and DOMILL?But more to the point there's an independent five-year study by the U.S. Department of Justice that is published to the public – please look it up as it's called, "Study of Deaths Following Electro Muscular Disruption" or look up the "Final Findings From the Expert Panel on the Safety of Conducted Energy Devices." You might even be surprised that TASER devices are the MOST studied less-lethal tool on an officers belt. The point is that while our technology isn't risk free it does save lives – more than 110,000 to date. With 107 countries using our technology it's not an unknown as there are now more than 1.93 million field uses as well as 1.4 million voluntary exposures. To infer there are unknown secrets behind TASER is dirty pool. Perhaps you should come clean.

 Oh the big, bad police, trying to protect themselves and the public against violent, aggressive scumbags.

28

How the Equality and Human Rights Commission forced the government's hand on stop and search

The Conservative party has long expressed strong support for an increase in the use of stop and search powers by the police, irrespective of the impact on community cohesion, and inequalities.

The Conservative party has long expressed strong support for an increase in the use of stop and search powers by the police, irrespective of the impact on community cohesion, and inequalities.

Now, Theresa May has backtracked and announced a six week consultation into the use of stop and search powers by police, after years of evidence that its application has disproportionately singled out ethnic minorities.

Police are able to use stop and search powers under the Police and Criminal Evidence Act (PACE) 1984. This Act is well known in marginalised black communities, and informing young people of their legal rights, as well as what to do if stopped, has long formed an essential part of the education of young people. There is even an app for it.

The Equality and Human Rights Commission (EHRC) commenced legal action against two police forces in 2010 due to this discriminatory practice. The action was suspended after a formal agreement and plan was made with the EHRC and the two forces to deal with the issue.

Three more forces, including the Metropolitan Police Service, voluntarily agreed a programme of reform to reduce race disproportionality in the application of stop and search to avert legal action by the EHRC. The outcomes of this work, Stop and Think Again, has been documented, demonstrating positive, fair outcomes are achievable.

This data clearly shows that black people were 4.6 times as likely to be stopped and searched by the Metropolitan Police as white people in 2009/10. Following the work of the EHRC, this has fallen to 3.7 black to white ratio in 201213.

There has been no corresponding fall in the white: Asian ratio and the EHRC have identified this as an area for further intervention.

When announcing the upcoming review, May told Parliament:

"We've all been told stories by constituents and members of the public about what it's like to be a young, law-abiding black man who has been stopped and searched by the police on more than one occasion."

The question is why have these 'stories' been permitted to blight the lives and dignity of young black males for so long; to damage community cohesion, and to fuel distrust in the police along race lines.

The EHRC is to be commended on this work, and the question that must be posed is whether Theresa May's hand was forced by the conclusion of the EHRC's report, in which they have pledged to:

"Continue to track progress in the forces whose action is covered in this report and to engage with them and further forces if and as appropriate"

Reader comments:

 The majority of street robberies in London are committed by young black males.

29

Ed Miliband should listen to Len McCluskey's real message

Len McCluskey, general secretary of Unite, has warned Ed Miliband of the need to keep Labour firmly on the left, in order to avoid defeat at the next general election. Specifically, Miliband has been advised by McCluskey to purge the shadow cabinet of its remaining Blairites, in the form of Jim Murphy, Douglas Alexander, and Liam Byrne.

Len McCluskey, general secretary of Unite, has warned Ed Miliband of the need to keep Labour firmly on the left, in order to avoid defeat at the next general election. Specifically, Miliband has been advised by McCluskey to purge the shadow cabinet of its remaining Blairites, in the form of Jim Murphy, Douglas Alexander, and Liam Byrne.

This has predictably led to claims of divisions in the Labour movement, and to accusations of disloyalty to the trades unions, particularly Unite, which was responsible for Ed Miliband's 2010 leadership victory. Unite is also Labour's biggest financial backer.

Keeping left

The left of the Labour movement strongly supported Ed Miliband, and it is nervous of signs that Ed will not follow through and deliver centre-left policies.

Ed Miliband was clear when he announced his shadow cabinet that it was drawn from "a broad range of talents across our party".

Until recently, he kept the door open to his brother David, even allegedly considering offering him Ed Ball's job. He has also in the past shown interest in listening to Tony Blair, perhaps until the latter's recent advice on the direction he thinks the Labour Party ought to head in so as to avoid becoming a party of protest.

What McCluskey is really doing is standing up for workers, particularly those in the now vilified public sector, whose rights have been dangerously eroded, and where roles have been stripped out of services such as the NHS, with very adverse impacts on services to patients. He is warning Ed Miliband not to develop an economic policy that simply echoes the coalition in a more palatable form ('austerity-lite'), because the public will see through it, and will not find it offers a sufficiently different alternative.

An alternative to 'austerity lite'

The interview given by Harriet Harman on the Andrew Marr Show in April is a signal of an 'austerity-lite' approach that McCluskey and many on the left fear. This interview was about trying on coalition clothes to see how they fit, and they were very ill-fitting indeed.

With such a hard line, Tory-led government in power, Labour needs to provide a strong alternative on the left, and the unions' traditional strength in protecting worker's rights is vital here. This is not about being 'red' as many working, formerly coping families are finding themselves pushed off the edge of a cliff. After all, in his One Nation Conference speech in 2012, Ed Miliband said this:

"I want to talk to all of the people of this country who always thought of themselves as comfortably off, but who now find themselves struggling to make ends meet. They ask: Why is it that when oil prices go up, the petrol price goes up. But when the oil price comes down, the petrol price just stays the same? They ask: Why is it that the gas and electricity bills just go up and up and up? And they ask: Why is it that the privatised train companies can make hundreds of millions of pounds in profit at the same time as train fares are going up by 10 per cent a year? They think the system just doesn't work for them."

Labour needs to be a strong opposition, and a good example is its pledge to reverse the NHS Health and Social Care Act. Further achievements will be ensuring that a growth programme for housing and jobs is central to economic policy.

There is nothing wrong with Ed, as leader of the Labour party, claiming the right to decide the direction of the party – indeed it is necessary – but this means listening to key players such as McCluskey. The fear of being labelled 'red' shouldn't drive the party to mimic the Tories; Miliband should find a way to identify a common discourse with McCluskey. The electorate will thank him for it in 2015.

Reader comments:

I strongly agree with Len McCluskey. am disappointed that Ed Miliband has chosen to attack him for wise counsel, and to listen instead to siren voices such as Liam Byrne, who fixed it for IDS for labour to abstain on the post-Pound land Jobseekers Bill vote.

The contrast between Ed's reaction to this and his reaction to the multiple attacks from Tony Blair and other Blairites speaks volumes.

This reminds me of the criticism of Kate (Dutchess of Cambridge) by Hilary Mantle. I know it sounds foolish, but I see parallels between this and Labour leaders who get used by the neoliberal machine (the finance industry and global corporations), to look like rock stars and flirt with the left, but end up delivering nothing for the 99% except more mortgage debt and economic bubbles.
The warning to Ed by Len is similar to the warning to Kate by Hilary Mantle, of course it provokes outrage, truthful criticism of value often will when we are living in a deluded world.
Hilary Mantle said she meant well, and I think Len did. If Ed Miliband has meant what he has said, he must know this. Only time will tell. It was wrong of him to say this was reprehensible.

30

Cameron needs to do more than attend the Stephen Lawrence memorial service to win the Black vote?

When Conservative councillor John Cherry spoke openly about his fear of Black and Minority Ethnic (BAME) children boarding weekly at a school in the West Sussex countryside, it was reminiscent of language that was not unusual in the 1980s and 1990s. The legacy of Stephen Lawrence's murder, 20 years ago, this month, was to trigger the Macpherson Inquiry, resulting in legislative reform that has driven out the worst such overt racist behaviour by those in public life.

When Conservative councillor John Cherry spoke openly about his fear of Black and Minority Ethnic (BAME) children boarding weekly at a school in the West Sussex countryside, it was reminiscent of language that was not unusual in the 1980s and 1990s.

The legacy of Stephen Lawrence's murder, 20 years ago, this month, was to trigger the Macpherson Inquiry, resulting in legislative reform that has driven out the worst such overt racist behaviour by those in public life.

Cherry resigned before the Conservative party could sack him. All the party then had to do was to distance itself from the views expressed. Cherry served on West Sussex County Council and Chichester Council, and both issued statements making it clear that the views he expressed were unacceptable and not representative of the views of their councils.

The actions of the two councils, in rejecting his statements, were driven by equality legislation that owes everything to the Lawrence case. There is a now a legal duty on councils to promote racial harmony and cohesion, act to promote equality, and act against discrimination.

Progress

Analysis of the impact of social and legislative change in the aftermath of the murder of Stephen Lawrence has rightly focused on the significant gains. The Macpherson Inquiry led to the broader recognition of institutional racism in British institutions and established an equality duty in the Equality Act 2010. The Single Race Equality Duty (now part of the Equality Act) has been law since 2001 as a direct outcome of Macpherson, and means that public bodies have a duty to protect people using their services, including staff, from discrimination on the grounds of race.

'Race' is often taken to be a characteristic only possessed by Black and Ethnic Minority (BAME) people, leading to resentment that a minority is receiving privileged protection. However, this legislation protects everyone as we all have an ethnicity, and can be discriminated against on this basis. So the legacy of Lawrence also protects white people from discrimination based on race.

The three leaders of the main political parties, as well as the Mayor of London, attended the Lawrence family memorial service. In light of the recent Conservative Party lurch to the right on immigration, Cameron's presence at the memorial service might, by some, be viewed as a part of a cynical campaign to recover some lost ground on the ethnic minority vote.

A cynical tactic to win votes?

The Tories have now embarked on a programme to increase its slice of the ethnic minority vote, which Labour has traditionally laid claim to, and this was seen in the outcome of the last general election.

Gavin Barwell, Tory MP for Croydon Central, described the approach the Conservative Party should take to attract Black voters, and hosted a talk at the progressive Tory Bright Blue pressure group recently on Race in Britain.

The Tories need to be more successful with the BAME population to win the next general election. The Party's campaign strategy must amount to more than attending the Lawrence memorial service to provide a good photo opportunity for Cameron and Johnson.However, their presence is a victory for the Lawrence family, and is testament to the campaigning stamina of Doreen and Neville Lawrence. In policing, education, public services, the voluntary and community sector, race inequality has a long journey ahead. Periodically, a John Cherry figure pops up and holds a sign post, signalling the long road that is still to be travelled.

Reader comments:

 "So Lawrence also protects white people from discrimination based on race." That's fine in theory, but, in reality, the state sector discriminates against white people all the time. Let's imagine that two people, one white and one non-white, go for a public sector job. They're more or less level in terms of qualifications, merit and overall suitability for the job. The non-white person will get the job every time. The white person has to be substantially ahead in terms of suitability to stand a chance. In the private sector, there will be a far fairer hiring process, because the employer's need is plainly and simply to get the best people available, in order to increase profits. I'm sure there are plenty out there saying, "You mustn't say that," but they'll have the devil's own job denying the truth of my statement.

By the way, how many racists (and other types of bigot) are there in the Labour party? Probably more than they'd care to admit. They're probably about level with the Tories for knuckle-dragging bigots, but Labour's knuckle-draggers are better at keeping their opinions to themselves. (Or does Labour benefit from a friendlier, more compliant, media?)

31

The musical backdrop to the backlash against Thatcherism

From the late 1970s Thatcherism ushered in an unexpectedly rich dimension of music-based protest and activism that pulled together youth movements from the very communities she sought to destroy.

From the late 1970s Thatcherism ushered in an unexpectedly rich dimension of music-based protest and activism that pulled together youth movements from the very communities she sought to destroy.

She dreaded a multicultural Britain, and instead of working to foster a harmonious future she worked against it, with devastating consequences in the 1980s. Here are three songs from young people in Britain at the time which showed communities suffering, but which also showed them pulling together.

The biggest Thatcher protest anthem in the pop charts was undoubtedly Stand down Margaret, from the Beat in 1982 (stay watching past the subtitles). The Band epitomised everything that Thatcher hated: multicultural working class youths, evidence of black immigration, and the struggling industrial communities of the Midlands. Their music fused their urban identifies with their struggle against Thatcher's Britain, producing a positive, uplifting sound.

Secondly Coventry band the Specials produced Ghost Town, which spelled out the consequences of Thatcherism on communities, jobs and society in 1981. A 2 Tone Records band – the label founded by Jerry Dammers – the groups was also a merger of black and white youth, performing side by side to symbolise the Britain Thatcher's government found unpalatable.

Finally, in 1981 Birmingham's UB40 recorded One in Ten, a song about being 'a statistic, a reminder of a world that doesn't care', in their mournful track about youth unemployment. A working class band of black and white youths, they showed that solidarity was possible between the members of the marginalised communities created by Thatcher's government.

Although these bands were too commercial for some tastes and went on to have huge popular and financial successes that took them away in some cases from the causes they had originally championed, they provided a vision of what could be.

The activities of the National Front were writ large in graffiti around the UK. It was bands like the Specials, UB40, the Beat, and the Selector which showed that a vision of respect, partnership and collaboration could grow between white British people and the Diaspora of the Commonwealth and Pakistan.

Reader comments:

I don't think the word 'multicultural' existed back then. I certainly never heard it used at the time, and I was in my mid-teens when the ska revival happened in 1979-1980. Multicultural Britain? No, only England has ever been multi-racial or multicultural. Non-white people are almost as rare as hens' teeth in the UK's other nations.
"Stand Down, Margaret", an LP track and B-side, was released in 1980 (I still have the 45, with "Best Friend" as the A-side) in my loft. Weren't The Specials a miserable lot? Yes, times were tough (nobody's denying that, although it was just as bad under Callaghan's government), but at least The Beat had a sense of humour, and more variety in their music.

This is not "evidence-based analysis" as your about page claims. The whole punk thing at the time was anti-Thatcher – the Angelic Upstarts released an album
called two million voices in 1981 when unemployment reached two million
for the first time. Anti-Pasti's No Government was actually No Maggie Thatcher and No Government. A lot by Crass was anti-Thatcher – take Sheep Farming in the Falklands or How Dos it Feel to be the Mother of 1,000 dead? And what about Billy Bragg?

Interesting that these examples come from the first 2-3 years when most of the problems would still have been caused by the economic policies of the previous government. It's like suggesting that punk was somehow a response to Thatcher (I have heard people say this). How about some songs from the late 80s (not Duran Duran, please).

My spouse and i don't think your own word 'multicultural' existed back then. My partner and i surely never heard The idea obtained with the time, AND ALSO i are inside MY mid teens As soon as your ska revival happened inside 1979-1980.
Multicultural Britain? No, Visit uçurtma single England offers ever been multiracial as well as multicultural. Non-white a person are almost Just like rare Just as hens' teeth in the UK's other nations. "Stand Down, Margaret", an LP track AND ALSO B-side, are introduced within 1980 (I still have your own 45, throughout "Best Friend" As ones A-side) throughout THE loft. Weren't your own Specials a great miserable lot? Yes, times were difficult (nobody's denying that, though This 'm As bad under Callaghan's government), but at the least ones Beat had a great sense regarding humour, ALONG WITH extra number inside it is music.

Wow what a great post. Thanks for sharing.

You have some really great posts and I feel I would be a good asset.
hay day cheats

32

Why did Kenyans elect a human rights abuser?

The Kenyan general election has been narrowly won by Uhuru Kenyatta, a man facing trial at the International Criminal Court for his alleged part in the killing of over a thousand people following the general election in 2007. The question must therefore be asked: why would a nation someone who stands accused of such crimes against humanity?

The son of Jomo Kenyatta, first president of Kenya, Uhuru faces trial in The Hague, accused of sponsoring and organising the devastating post-election violence in 2007. His running mate William Ruto faces the same charge.

The question must therefore be asked: why would a nation elect two candidates who stand accused of such crimes against humanity?

After victory in the 2007 elections was awarded to Mwai Kibaki, homes were set alight in the Kibera slum region during the swearing in ceremony in protest at the outcome of the election, sparking violence that led to the deaths and displacement of thousands of people.

The election outcome was disputed, and Kenyan and international observers claimed there was widespread vote-rigging.

To secure justice for the victims, the initial plan was for proceedings to be held in Kenya, on a Truth and Reconciliation basis, in order to avoid inflaming the inter-ethnic sensitivities that characterised the political violence after the 2007 elections.

The Waki report set out the options for getting justice for the victims. The government declined to have domestic hearings, leaving the ICC as the only option.

Kenyans, still suffering the aftermath of the injustices in the post election period in 2007, and genuinely wanting justice, supported the plan for ICC prosecutions and expected those accused to be found guilty.

The first possible explanation for Kenyatta's win is the claim is that the facts about the ICC indictment has been kept from the Kenyans, with Kenyatta and Ruto giving the electorate the message that the indictments are about ethnic persecution by the European court.

The second potential explanation is the perceived power relations, and past colonial relations between Europe and Africa so that many Kenyans have now been persuaded to think of the charges from the ICC as being about western interference in Africa's continuing journey toward political and stability in the post-colonial world.

Kenya's sensitivity to the role played by the British government has moved the latter to reassure the Kenyan people that it only operates at arm's length, and with relevant approvals.

Kenyatta therefore has given his nation the clear message that it is the country's political processes, and in particular the post-election processes of 2007, rather than criminal behaviour by him as in individual, that is on trial.

Clearly only half of the population bought this as the vote only narrowly avoided a run-off vote, with the Kenyatta/Ruto ticket only securing 50.07 per cent of the vote and with the nearest opponent, Raila Odinga, claiming vote-rigging in this election and vowing to seek a legal review of the voting processes.

Kenyatta's victory also means western governments will be reluctant to deal with the new government given the ambiguity over the culpability of the President.

Kenyans are still licking their wounds after the 2007 elections and want to move forward. So here was an opportunity to do just that, to cast Kenyatta and Ruto to their fate, if they are culpable, and move on with a stable government process.

But the Kenyans voting for Kenyatta and Ruto feel they will be getting just that, as they do not believe the two will be found guilty.

The trial in The Hague starts in July, and both the president-elect and the deputy president-elect will plead not guilty.

Reader comments:

There are plenty of other human rights abusers ruling nations in the UN as well as this guy. The more important question is why we don't clear the stables at the UN?

Then we wouldn't face the shambles of punk states like Communist Cuba lecturing the West on human rights abuses. 'Oooo but they have such clean tap water', say leftists! Google WORLD REPORT 2012 CUBA HUMAN RIGHTS WATCH.

This is entirely misleading!

Note, The election was NOT "narrowly won by Uhuru Kenyatta". It was won by a margin of about 800,000 votes to the closest rival. Is someone still hopping there will be chaos in Kenya so that they can get 'juicy' news????

And our leaders are they not human rights abusers or is it different when its the other side of the world?

33

Are the South African police to blame for the murder of Reeva Steenkamp?

The South African police, and the government have a lot of injustices and failures that can be laid at their door, but the actions of Oscar Pistorius on Valentine's Day is not one of them.

Henke Pistorius, father of Oscar, recently linked the killing of the model Reeva Steenkampf to alleged failings by the South African police, the ANC government, and to violent crime by black South Africans. He told the Telegraph that these factors combined to compel South Africans to arm themselves for protection.

Pistorius senior is clearly clutching at straws to explain what could have led to the disastrous decision taken by Oscar to blindly shoot at an 'unseen would-be assailant' in his bathroom, as he claims happened, who turned out to be Reeva.

The implication is that the fear of crime is so high that everyone, particularly wealthy white South Africans, is trigger-happy.

Henke's nonsensical claims, probably commonly held in white farming communities, are not borne out in official statistics, which show a steady fall in most crimes, including violent crime.

Over an eight year period, South African police statistics show that contact crime (murder, attempted murder, sexual offences, assault, GBH, common assault, and aggravating & common robbery) has fallen by 35.5 per cent.

Oscar's father points to the high levels of murders of white farmers in robberies, as a further reason for the very high levels of gun ownership in South Africa.

Calls for these murders to be awarded a special crime category, or even regarded as white genocide, have been rejected by South African police, who deny that they are race-based murders or have a hate element.

The extreme brutality of these murders is not just a hallmark of the farm murders, but of violent crime in general in South Africa.

The use of these factors to justify heavy gun ownership by the Pistorius family, evidently for leisure and protection, is a smokescreen to mask the very big questions Oscar will have to find answers to in his murder trial.

The wider Pistorius family have now rejected Henke's comments, which are not borne out by the evidence and cast a negative light on the black population, itself still struggling in post Apartheid South Africa.

The perception of a vulnerable, white wealthy community, forced to live barricaded in gated settings, to fend off a constant onslaught of violent crime by black people is a picture South Africa does not recognise.

The fears of the international community when the football World Cup was awarded in 2010 was based on such scaremongering, but were proved unfounded with the delivery of a largely crime free tournament.

The South African police, and the government have a lot of injustices and failures that can be laid at their door, but the actions of Oscar Pistorius on Valentine's Day is not one of them.

Reader comments:

A man shoots and kills a woman and the blame is directed at the police. Remove the guns and take responsibility for your actions.

Henke. You have the money. You have a passport. Apply for citizenship elsewhere. Leave SA, and never come back. You are no patriot.

I'm glad some leftists are finally opening their eyes to the savagery going on down there, the second article I've seen in days. I never knew leftists had it in them.

But can we expect leftists to go further than criticising the police, which is familiar to the comfort zone? Or will they go further and admit it's the inbuilt prejudices of the ANC itself which inevitably led to brutality and totalitarianism.

The comments here highlighted much: http://www.leftfoot-forward.org/2013/03/why-are-south-african-police-mimick-ing-white-supremacists-mido-macia/

But then, the violent ANC was headed by bullying Marxist, Gaddaffi-wooing terrorist who stayed in jail because he refused to renounce violence. So scenes were set.

 Many hate crimes are being committed against the white minority. The government denies that any single such a crime was ever committed by any black racist. Many people in government believe in BLT which wrongly suggests blacks are incapable of racism. I say, if true that would make blacks superior to human beings...

The SA governor is a black nationalist government that will do anything in order to hide the extend and brutality of black racism and the effect of hate crimes on minorities. (Sadly they are white and not PC enough)

 A very simplistic take on South Africa. Most people just don't have any idea...

 Yes, indeed, you're trying to bring the murders here. You're trying to bring the brutality and savagery which you praise so much here. You are the one wanting a race war.

 Though at least you admit the ANC are capable of murder. They did have a terrorist section after all.

 You're trying to control me and what I feel and think again. And keep talking about something completely different to your support for the NP.

 Anarchists live in a black-and-white, either-or world. I criticise the ANC, there fore I automatically support the NP. That's one reason anarchists frighten the public.

 You're trying to push your worldview onto other people again, demanding they share it, or else. Far right thugs like you scare a lot of people. The mindset of the NF enforcers who you resemble...

To criticise isn't to push. Anarchists can push, as many a riot cop who's been attacked with bricks and bottles can testify.

 Yes, of course you're going to try and false flag your attacks again. And that makes your push less excusable, doesn't it.

34

Why are South African police mimicking white supremacists?

The sickening killing of 27-year-old Mido Macia in South Africa this week brought to mind the white supremacist murders in the US which amounted to 'lynchings'. This, together with the recent high profile rape and murder of Anene Booysen - and even the Oscar Pistorius case - point to a latent violence in the country that the government seems reluctant to tackle.

The sickening killing of 27 year old Mido Macia in South Africa this week brought to mind the white supremacist murders in the US which amounted to 'lynchings'.

James Byrd Jr, a black man, was tied to the back of a pickup truck in Texas in 1998 by three men, two of whom were confirmed white supremacists, and dragged at speed to a gruesome death.

As recently as 2010, Anthony Hill, also a black man, was dragged almost ten miles by a white male after being shot, and the matter is now being investigated as a hate crime.

Such killings are the ultimate demonstration of control, power, contempt and hate for the victim.

But in post-Apartheid South Africa, where the police are black, the world, and the people hoped and perhaps dreamed of better.

Black people, who suffered grievously at the hands of the South African police under Apartheid, have a right to expect better. But sadly the corrupting influence of power seems to have transcended racial solidarity in the killing of Macia.

To see black policemen mimic the racist modus operandi of white supremacists is particularly galling. It also sends a clear message to poor blacks that "we are your masters now".

The brutal video shows that there is good coordination between the policemen who rapidly tether Macia to their vehicle and are chillingly coordinated in their actions. It does not look like the first time they have done it; they appear much practiced in this form of torture and humiliation.

In South Africa, violence is always bubbling just beneath the surface; and when race, poverty, and power are added to the equation things can quickly boil over, as seen in the massacre of Marikana miners of 2012.

As with that atrocity, an investigation has been announced following public outcry, with remarks of condemnation from Jacob Zuma.

The recent high profile rape and murder of Anene Booysen – and even the Oscar Pistorius case – point to a latent violence in the country that the government seems reluctant to tackle in a systematic way. It is time for South Africa to join the dots and see the bigger picture.

Reader comments:

 Interesting perception from the outside looking in. Fascist Police States are not the sole preserve of "Whitesupremists," and if the author knew more of our History, they would knowabout Shaka. By today's standard looking back, Shaka was a Fascist Dictator and Shaka's Rock still stands. Further north Robert Mugabe still commits crimes against his own people. And there once was a man called Idi Amin, and then there was Charles Taylor. Power mad psycopaths come in all shapes, sizes and colours. It is not the sole preserve of one race group or another.

 Quite a revelation to many leftists who only think in terms of 'rednecks and Nazis' when waffling about the brutal beatings of who we would call minorities. Brutal tyrannies in Africa seem pretty much par for the course but what judders the leftist brain to a standstill is that this happens in South Africa – a place where, doctrine states, the ANC rainbow nation has brought peace and prosperity and equality.

In fact, crime cripples the nation, along with poverty and scapegoating against whites. Though with Nelson Mandela a Marxist terrorist leader whose wife set fire to political opponents, it looked from the outset a case of one flawed man versus an establishment of other flawed men whilst riding the vehicle of liberation.

Talk about life under apartheid, eh.

http://edition.cnn.com/2008/WORLD/africa/06/10/safrica.mmm/index.html

ANC racism. Yup, heard that right: http://za.news.yahoo.com/anc-most-racist-party-024053065.html

http://www.telegraph.co.uk/health/healthnews/9280481/More-than-half-of-South-Africas-children-live-in-poverty.html

Nelsy: http://www.netcomuk.co.uk/~springbk/enemy.html

Agreed. And i suggest all the celebrities and liberal free-dom-lovers who cheered Mandela and the ANC's rise now come together to protest the likes of the ANC's approval of Mugabe's racist persecution of white farmers:

http://www.guardian.co.uk/world/2003/jan/11/zimbabwe.andrewmeldrum

I'll drink to the Left come that day.

Its the collateral damage of any uprising, conflict or power struggle, regardless of whether morally right or wrong. The collapse of Apartheid, Communism and the Arab Dictator-ships were all morally right, but the inevitable fallout and trauma and psychological damage will continue for many many decades to come, and affect everyone.

It would be a mistake to suppose that the South African police force was all white before apartheid. For obvious reasons – you could hardly go undercover in the townships if you were a white officer – and for more subtle ones too, many of the rank and file police were black. The brutality and impunity of the police force seems to have continued under a political system which has not changed that much, although the skin colour of some of those at the top has. I'm not knocking the massive improvement that the end of the apartheid system and all its appalling absurdity has brought, but essentially it is still a capitalist, sexist, violent and extremely unequal country.

 That's right. It's good to see the baddies go. However, totalitarian Islamic dictatorships remain. In fact, they've be re-instated in places like Egypt and even fueled by the very Muslim Brotherhood which Obama, of all people, allies with and employs at home. We're not out of the tunnel yet.

 Correctly, there is massive outrage when the Davey ton #SAPS dragged a Mozambican taxi driver to his death behind a police van — in a clearly #xenophobic hate crime www. http://youtube.com/watch?v=xnLNX_UbuHowever why the deafening silence whenever whites are killed that way? I archive the hate crimes in SA since 1994 and have many such 'dragging deaths' on record: such as this young dad, dragged to his death #Farmer pic.twitter.com/tfCEpkxUaY

 Re: the James Byrd dragging case – James Byrd was not an innocent black man as is always implied – he was a criminal who had abused his later executioner in jail. White men in black-majority jails join white racist gangs for their own protection, otherwise they will become the sex-slave and "bitch" of a black. For most black men, prison is no hardship at all – free food, clothing, medical, gym, and the opportunity to attack whites with impunity.

 In South Africa it's long past the collateral stage. If Americans truly know the barbarism going on South Africa would be constant in the news. What is happening in South Africa and the reason for extreme violence is because of the country going through a revolution changing it into a Marxist communist country. Google NDR which stands for national democratic revolution. Google it. Coming to a State near you.

 Indeed. And I think it's partly stayed that way because the huge media and political focus on South Africa was eased after the regime ended Apartheid. Despite appearances, the new regime has, shall we say, its own deep flaws and prejudices. Give the Left credit, they're fantastic noise makers but I think they'll need to be bullied into harassing the 'right' oppressors. (Indeed, the tone of this article reads between the lines as

'Wow, the light and the way brigade are lowering themselves to act like the lowdown whites? Who'd've thunk it?')

'lynchings' were far and few in between, white criminals, black criminals, any criminals begat that fate. The common denominator was the depravity of the crime. It was the communities swift justice, black communities as well as white communities exercised that right. It wasn't until a deviant Jew in Atlanta committed a horrific savage rape/murder of a little girl it became a big deal. Despite the inhumane cruelty and overwhelming evidence the Jews defended the perp with all they had. Even to the point of prolonged retrials attempting to incite racial hatred trying to pin it on a mentally deficient black man who happened to be a janitor at the scene of the crime. The "stupid rednecks" did not buy it, and that jew tactic failed. The final attempt was long delays until the outrage of the crime subsided as they plotted their 30 pieces of silver into a newly financially supported governor's pen in the form of a pardon.

The system of fair trial was being usurped leaving the community (black and white) with no alternative but to exercise their right to swift justice. The Jewish struggle for the right of the self-proclaimed "chosen" to be a minority ruling a majority started the campaign the State 'has the supreme right against the individual' removing justice out of the peoples hands firmly into the courts hands. Experience has taught them those hands could be tied, manipulated, and laden with gold subject to their whim.

They then took a 2 prong attack by first creating and controlling the NAACP, reviving and controlling a perverted version of the old defunct Ku Klux Klan. This enabled their subversive expertise of creating a series of Hegelian dialectics through racial differences into conflicts. Their many leftists organizations were designed to create reactionaries culminating in the left-right paradigm, much easier to control and set the terms of national debate. Hence the Pavlov dog reaction to the term lynching, the Jew transgressions are absent leaving only a white-black confrontation.

35

How far back should retrospective government apologies go?

Now that Enda Kenny has apologised to the victims of the Magdalene laundries scandal in Ireland, Claudia Tomlinson asks how far back retrospective government apologies should go.

Now that Enda Kenny has apologised to the victims of the Magdalene laundries scandal in Ireland, which saw thousands of women with social problems detained and used for forced labour, the question of the value of such apologies can be examined.

Between 1922 and 1996, approximately 10,000 women and girls suffered degrading, humiliating and abusive treatment at the hands of the Catholic nuns who ran the institutions. The value of this apology to the victims, and survivors, who often experience long term trauma symptoms, is unlimited.

The wrongdoing they experienced can be alleviated through the act of a nationally authoritative figure validating their experience.

As with many parliamentary apologies for historical abuses that are either government-sponsored or where the government is clearly complicit, this national apology had to be dragged out reluctantly from the Irish government.

What are the reasons, then, for this reluctance?

Of course, sitting governments do not want to be held accountable for acts that it was not directly responsible for, particularly if the act took place when a different party was in power. Compensation payments can be considerable, and in this case, the government has rightly agreed they can be paid to survivors to cover the cost of counselling, and welfare services.

An apology for a historical wrong can also jeopardise a government's current political standing, however the incumbent Fine Gael- Labour coalition government should mean the risk is shared between the two parties, thus increasing their willingness to apologise.

What are the benefits to governments in making national apologies for historical wrongs, and why are apologies made in some instances and not others?

David Cameron has issued several apologies on behalf of the British government in a relatively short time in office. The first followed the publication of the Bloody Sunday shortly after becoming prime minister.

He then apologised to the families of the Hillsborough disaster, and more recently for the suffering and neglect at the Mid-Staffordshire NHS Foundation Trust, after the publication of the Francis Inquiry report.

All of these apologies were issued on behalf of the government.

The gusto with which Cameron delivered them can leave no doubt that he is confident about the political benefit for himself and his party, given the grandeur of the gestures.

So is sorry no longer the hardest word? How far back should governments go? What about international historical abuses?

No doubt sitting governments will seek to draw the line somewhere as, given the adventures of the British government overseas in the last two hundred years alone, David Cameron would spend every Wednesday lunchtime repenting at the dispatch box.

Reader comments:

Surry's always the hardest word, at least when apologising for all your own crap. Tony Blair also repeatedly apologised for the natural potato famine, so lefties know of what they speak when they ask if enough is enough. And as for 'adventures of the British government', that's who it was by: the government. Though when we see school curricula today, kids are always made to feel ashamed for the behaviour of a political elite-endorsed crust of dictators which crushed their own ancestors – black or white. A tangent really, but tell the likes of Diane Abbott it's not the rest of us who can play divide and conquer!

 No, wait, how about apologising for allowing Islamic immigration?

36

Net closing on Canadian PM as key ally resigns

The resignation of the Canadian minister for aboriginal affairs leaves prime minister Steve Harper more exposed to criticism over the country's treatment of the aboriginal community.

John Duncan, minister for aboriginal affairs in Canada, has been surviving on borrowed time since 2011 when the community of Attawapiskat jarred the conscience of the country with its deplorable housing conditions.

He embarrassed Conservative prime minister Stephen Harper by claiming to have no knowledge of what was happening until the Red Cross was called in to the north-eastern territory.

So his resignation late on Friday (15 February) – just before a long weekend – was Harper's attempt to bury a bombshell.

The reason given for the resignation was due to Duncan writing a character reference to the Tax Court on behalf of a constituent in 2011, clearly a conflict of interest given his ministerial role, so this is being viewed as a cover for the inevitable.

There have been calls for his resignation on the grounds of his incompetence in his ministerial brief, which sparked off the Idle No More Indigenous People's movement last year, and which saw demonstrations and rail blockades.

Idle No More appears to have lost focus, however, and many opponents claimed a lack of organisation and cohesion of purpose, which is being used to further discredit the project.

Although the organisation is yet to issue a formal press release in response to Duncan's departure, the movement's leaders and supporters have been clear, via Twitter at least, that this is a welcome development.

If Duncan's departure was so low key in its significance to the government, why, for example, did Harper attempt to bury it?

As it immediately trended on Twitter, the attempt was not successful, and suggested a higher level of significance to Canadians than Harper has probably hoped.

There have already been calls for Harper's resignation over the government's mishandling of Indigenous People's issues during the course of the past year, and now that Duncan has gone, anger can be more directly focused on the prime minister.

Duncan's departure is the second recent high profile casualty suffered by Harper's government. Senator Patrick Brazeau, an indigenous opponent of Idle No More and a former chief of the Congress of Aboriginal Peoples (CAP), was suspended by the government following allegations of assault.

CAP represents off-reserve Aboriginals, and has not suffered the severe disadvantage as experienced by those living on reserve, the focus of Idle No More. Brazeau was someone Conservatives could rely on to support Harper's divide and rule agenda, and has previously mocked his own people.

With these two gone, Harper's judgement is increasingly being called into question on the issue of indigenous issues, and Canadians from across the political spectrum are joining the dots.

37

Report into scandal hit Mid-Staffs NHS Trust could have 'radical implications'

Robert Francis QC will publish his report tomorrow on the public inquiry into the commissioning, supervisory and regulatory bodies responsible for the failed Mid-Staffordshire NHS Foundation Trust. This will be the fifth review of the systemic failures in the trust between 2005 and 2008.

Commencing with the Healthcare Commission's report and ending with the upcoming second Francis report in February, the findings amount to the what will be widely regarded as the worst failing of care provided by the NHS.

Francis's first report, published in 2010, looked at the care provided by the trust, and was commissioned by then health secretary, Andy Burnham.

It found that patients suffered considerably during the period under investigation, suffering degrading continence care, poor personal hygiene and worrying safety issues such as falls leading to serious injuries.

There was also severe neglect in the provision of nutrition and hydration, as well as a failure to provide meals and water to patients, or to support patients to eat the meals with drinks placed out of their reach.

Evidence of low standards of cleanliness and hygiene and infection control was also uncovered.

One of the key recommendations from the inquiry was that there should be an investigation into the regulatory bodies supervising Mid-Staffs during the period, as none had picked up on the difficulties. The latest report into the Trust, out tomorrow (6th February), is a full public inquiry – as ordered by Andrew Lansley in 2010 – into the reasons why the oversight bodies saw nothing wrong.

The current chief executive of the NHS, Sir David Nicholson, who was chief executive of the Strategic Health Authority responsible for the trust, has faced calls for his resignation, but feels he has a role to play in implementing the recommendations of the latest inquiry.

Patients at the trust have continued to suffer poor treatment, and only recently the case of the baby found with a dummy taped to its face made headlines.

Mid-Staffs chief executive's January 2013 report to the trust board shows that Monitor, the healthcare regulator, has declared the Trust both clinically and financially unsustainable, meaning it is likely to be subject to the Unsustainable Provider Regime.

This could mean it is subject to a 'failure regime' and broken up and taken over by other trusts.

The political context, cuts, staff morale, and the role played by the media are all likely to be part of the picture when the report of the public inquiry is published, and the recommendations are expected to have wide ranging and radical implications for NHS reforms.

38

How will UK patients benefit from Healthcare UK?

The government this week launched Healthcare UK, in Dubai at the Arab Health Congress, seeking to sell the best of the UK health sector to rich markets around the world. The NHS, the private sector, and academic health centres of excellence are to be branded and sold as world leaders in healthcare excellence.

It is claimed this venture will bring income to the NHS, jobs and growth for our struggling economy and no one will suggest this is not badly needed.

However, the first question that must be asked is whether the UK health sector is sufficiently stable to tolerate a distraction and what are the real benefits to be derived by ordinary local UK NHS trusts?

An example of this venture is Kings Health Partners, a partnership of Guys and St Thomas's Hospital, Kings College Hospital, South London and Maudsley NHS Foundation Trust, and Kings College London.

The Department of Health has listed Kings Health Partners as a recent example of a public health organisation delivering the type of contracts to be sought under Healthcare UK in its work in developing services in Burjeel Hospital, and Shining Towers, wealthy facilities both in Abu Dhabi.

Kings Health Partners is developing a Foetal Medicine Clinic at Burjeel Hospital, Abu Dhabi and setting up a Day Case Outpatient Department in Shining Towers, Abu Dhabi.

Earlier analysis of the idea of Healthcare UK shows the focus is clearly on exploiting the reputation of NHS centres of excellence to capitalise on opportunities in rich countries that have traditionally sent patients abroad for treatment and are now seeking to set up their own local care centres.

There is a risk a two-tier service in the NHS will develop with increasingly prestigious and well known NHS organisations being supported to meet the demands of rich international customers. They will outstrip the offer to patients from local hospitals that will not have such support and provide such 'excellence'.

Further, how will the current significant turbulence in the UK health sector be parcelled up at the trade fair in Dubai? Will there be any awkward questions asked about the 25,000 who marched last week against the shambles that is emerging in the NHS in south east London?

Most importantly, how will the income from providing healthcare to the fabulously wealthy flow back into the UK to fund care to populations and improve the health of the nation, particularly the poorest?

Kings Health Partners is one of the few publicly funded organisations listed by the Department of Health as recently embarking on delivery of these lucrative contracts; most are private companies.

It is only after the details of the initiative are fully unveiled in Abu Dhabi that the intentions can be evaluated, but public organisations setting out on this journey will need to retain an awareness of an earlier example that outlines the advantages private companies have when competing with public agencies.

Whilst most people using healthcare services in the UK probably do not desire the opulence of the Burjeel Hospital, neither do they wish to lose basic services or see deterioration in existing services due to the cuts and undeliverable demands of the current NHS reforms.

Addressing these issues would be seen by many as a greater priority than Healthcare UK.

Reader comments:

 Which UK health sector do you mean? As I understand it, Scotland's NHS is quite close to what Nye Bevan envisaged, with Wales' and Northern Ireland's systems not far from that point. It's only England's NHS that has experienced significant privatisation. It's only English taxpayers who get so little bang for their buck, despite paying the most. Please don't try to give the impression that there is one standard pan-UK NHS, because there hasn't been such a beast for many years.

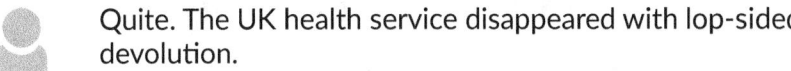

Quite. The UK health service disappeared with lop-sided devolution.
How strange a far-left website would support a Tory led government in the lie that NHS uk still exists.

'what are the real benefits to be derived by ordinary local UK NHS trusts?' There is no such thing as a UK NHS Trust. There are English NHS Trusts. In Scotland Trusts were abolished in 2004. Scotland has NHS Health Boards so does Wales. If the author doesn't even know that then what the hell is she doing writing an article?

To be fair to the poster, the name Healthcare UK was cooked up by this Conservative government. You are right about the devolved nature of the NHS, and the poster was at fault for depending too much on the government's Press Releases which also speaks of "the UK's health sector". I suspect that the government are looking at how various universities have opened campuses abroad and figure that hospitals can do that too. The two are very different of course, not least because in England students have to pay and hence higher education is now a business thanks to Tony Blair.

39

Idle No More – Canada's indigenous citizens fight for their rights

Canada is an extremely beautiful country, regularly featuring in lists of the best places in the world to live. Along with Australia, and New Zealand, it is a popular emigration destination for the British people, along with others from around the world.

But it also has an ugly, hidden underbelly, one that you will not see in its promotional videos designed to boost its already booming tourist industry.

The story of indigenous people: the First Nations, the Inuits, and Métis, is one of poverty, unemployment, slum housing, high crime, mental illness, substance misuse (particularly alcohol abuse), and poor educational attainment.

Only 8 per cent of indigenous people obtain a university degree compared with 23% of non-indigenous people, and 34% of working age adults between 25 and 64 years of age, have not completed a high school diploma, according to the 2006 Canadian Census, Ottawa.

From the 1880s, the indigenous people of Canada suffered what is commonly regarded as genocide through the deaths of approximately 50,000 First Nations children compulsorily taken from their families and communities and placed in government residential schools.

Those that did not die suffered brutal lives of physical and sexual abuse, under the auspices of the Catholic Church, which sought to impose a curriculum which forbade the speaking of aboriginal languages, or any cultural practice – in other words a forced process of assimilation into mainstream, Eurocentric cultural ideals.

The last of these schools closed in 1996, and following the establishment of a Truth and Reconciliation Commission, prime minister Stephen Harper, in Parliament, issued an apology to the Aboriginal people.

In December 2012, communicated largely through the social media of blogging, Twitter, and Facebook, the Idle No More campaign was born, and has spread rapidly throughout Canada, with awareness raised in America, Europe, and beyond. Although it was sparked by the passage of legislation in December that will impact the land rights and historical treaties of indigenous peoples, the activism was a very long time in the making.

The Arab uprisings and the Occupy movement appear to have seeped into the consciousness of indigenous Canadians to precipitate this action.

A year ago, Canada was shamed on an international stage when the Red Cross had to step in to bring relief during a humanitarian crisis in the First Nation community of Attawapiskat. Poverty, deprivation, substandard and overcrowded housing, and poor sanitation in Attawapiskat is the story of many reserves in Canada.

Conservative prime minister Stephen Harper promptly accused the reserve management of budgetary mismanagement and the Minister for Aboriginal Affairs appointed a third party manager to oversee the reserve's finances. This was successfully challenged in court by the reserve Chief, Theresa Spence.

Idle No more has been a phenomenally successful campaign of grassroots activism involving demonstrations, flash mobs in Toronto's Eaton Centre, rail blockades, and drawing the attention of the international media. The centrepiece of the campaign is the hunger strike of Chief Theresa Spence, started on December 11th, demanding a meeting with Premier Stephen Harper.

Opposition MPs have visited her, and she has been offered and declined a meeting with the incompetent Minister for Aboriginal Affairs, John Duncan.

Academic, lawyer and First Nation activist Pam Palmater, is one of the driving forces behind the media campaign and vows the campaign will continue to grow and escalate until the demands of Idle No More are met; for Stephen Harper, the stakes are high and his stance of refusing to meet face to face with leaders of the campaign, and instead threatening the rule of law, means there are surely turbulent times ahead for Canada, on the road to Indigenous Justice.

40

The Marikana massacre: a search for the truth

The Marikana massacre resulted in the deaths of 69 protesters, allegations of corruption, and appalling behaviour from businesses.

The African National Congress (ANC) marked the first 100 years of its existence in 2012. This proud milestone was marred by what is widely regarded as the modern day Sharpeville massacre, and resulted in chilling reverberations from the past. In 1960, the South African police opened fire, shot and killed 69 black protesters in an internationally condemned act. There were many allegations the protesters had provoked the police and were to blame. The 21st of March, the day of the massacre in 1960, is a national holiday to recognise and pay tribute to those who laid down their lives for the freedom many in South Africa now experience.

It was therefore bitter news that in 2012, we are confronted with the massacre of 34 black protesting mineworkers, killed by the South African police, in August this year, in Rustenburg, north-east of Johannesburg.

The ANC was invigorated in the 1940s by the passion, belief, commitment and dedication of Oliver Tambo, Walter Sisulu, and Nelson Mandela, and their liberation movement culminating in the overthrowing of the internationally despised system of Apartheid in 1994. The only surviving member of this trio, Mandela, is now ill in hospital aged 94, and the faithful around the world hopes he recovers.

Workers at the Lonmin platinum mine went on strike for better wages and eventually secured an increase of 22%. The cost was 10 people dead, including two police officers and two security guards, on the 10th August, and 34 miners shot dead by police on the 16th August.

There was international disbelief when, in the immediate

aftermath, 270 miners were arrested and charged with the murders, although these charges were eventually dropped by the National Prosecution Authority, the state prosecutor. It was widely reported South African police participated in creating an illusion tribal weapons had been used by the protestors on each other, by positioning these weapons next to the bodies of the killed miners.

Jacob Zuma and the ANC quickly came under suspicion of political interference in affairs of state prosecution. He also stood accused of gross insensitivity about the loss of life, and lack of solidarity with poor black workers. His subsequent announcement of a week of national mourning was regarded as a cynical gesture to placate a concerned international community. His lamentable actions led to dissent within the ANC, and calls for his removal from office.

The role of the two rival trades unions is also under examination. The National Mineworkers Union (NUM) threatened by newcomer Association of Mineworkers and Construction Union (Amcu), and this is seen as contributing to the unrest in the period immediately preceding the shootings.

Lonmin stands accused of exploitation of its 28,000 mineworkers. There are claims squalid living and working conditions are endured by the mineworkers, whilst Lonmin reaps huge profits.

Lonmin's claims of significant investment in the community and families, and its package of support for bereaved families, was seen as meagre compared with its demands for the workers to get back to work shortly after the tragedy, in order to minimise lost profits. In the view of many, Lonmin bears a lot of responsibility for the tragedy.

When the dust settled, Zuma announced a Commission of Inquiry, which commenced on the 1st October, led by retired judge Ian Farlan. The Marikana Inquiry will look at the role of Lonmin and whether it acted to resolve the industrial dispute responsibly, or whether its actions contributed to sustaining tensions with the workers. The inquiry will examine the role of conflict between the two competing unions and whether their rivalry contributed to the incident. Lastly, the inquiry will probe the role of the police response.

An emergence of anxiety about the exclusion of the voices of the ordinary miners from the Marikana inquiry prompted sociologist Professor Peter Alexander, in collaboration with researchers Thapelo Lekowa, Botsang Mmope, Luke Sinwell and Bongani Xeswi, to write a book about the killings.

The book is the result of interviews conducted with the strikers, carried out on the mountain close to the massacre of 16th August. Entitled "Marikana, a view from the mountain and a case to answer", the book offers the perspective of those who lived through the experience; on the other hand, the Farlan inquiry, the 'official' perspective, must deliver the truth and justice must be done, and be seen to be done.

Last week, the ANC conference opened, to give delegates the opportunity to elect the top leadership positions in the party, ahead of the 2014 election. It remains to be seen what impact Marikana will play in the outcomes of the leadership elections

41

Will the Marikana Inquiry Halt the Violence on Its Own Doorstep to Deliver the Truth?

When Jacob Zuma announced a Commission of Inquiry to investigate the shooting dead of 34 black miners by South African police, many felt it was intended to divert attention from the avalanche of criticism directed at him and his Government in the aftermath of the massacre. Few observers of the Inquiry proceedings, since it started in October 2012, felt it would deliver anything but a protective shield for the authorities. If the Commission reports what is widely believed to be the full truth underlying the events, it will be highly commended.

Following strike action for increased pay and improved working conditions, 34 miners working at the Lonmin mine, were killed in Rustenburg, on 16 August, and a further 10 died in incidents in the previous period. The Inquiry was commissioned to look at the factors that caused the incidents, and the role played by the police, the mine owners, the mining unions, and the mine workers in the massacre.

Shortly after the opening of the Inquiry, sociologist Peter Alexander led a team of academics and researchers that conducted its own interviews with mine workers and other witnesses on the mountain where the massacre took place. They published: 'Marikana a view from the mountain and a case to answer', which builds a case that assigns responsibility to both the South African Government, and the police. This work was motivated by conviction that the Inquiry would not listen to the voices of ordinary miners.

Inquiry proceedings have been hit by numerous crises which are seen as undermining the delivery of truth and justice by the Inquiry. The support to the families of the deceased miners during the Inquiry has been poor, and led to their absence at the start of the proceedings. Initial financial state support, on humanitarian grounds was soon withdrawn, leaving the impoverished families of survivors to fund themselves as best they could. A request from the legal team representing many of the families, and injured survivors to move the location of the Commission from Rustenburg to Pretoria to ease the financial burden on the families was not granted as members of the local community did want to be denied access. However, in a positive move, President Zuma has authorised the Commission to hold some of its hearings at any location.

Violence and death has also been a backdrop to the proceedings. In April this year, Dali Mpofu, the lawyer representing the miner's families, and those who were arrested after the massacre, was seriously injured when stabbed by an unknown assailant. The Commission took the view that his attack, which he survived, was unconnected to his work role in the Inquiry, to which he has been able to return.

The branch secretary of the National Union of Mine workers, Daluvuyo Bongo was killed last year before he could testify at the Commission, and a traditional healer who attended the miners, was also killed earlier this year.

The Inquiry has also been shaken by two apparent suicides of survivors of the massacre, the most recent taking place in May. A young miner, 27-year-old Lungani Mabutyana, was found hanging from a tree after an earlier suicide attempt due to financial worries.

A further death, this time of Mawethu Khululekile Steven, a leader of the Association of Mine workers and Construction Union (AMCU) has also happened this month, before his testimony to the Inquiry has taken place. In what appeared to be a targeted killing, the union leader was shot four times by assailants who entered the bar he was in.

The Inquiry will continue hearing evidence until 31 May, and then has six weeks to submit its report to Zuma. Its findings must be truthful, meaningful, just, and pave the way for reconciliation and improved conditions for South Africa's mine workers. Until then, the Commission must do more to halt the violence and killings on its own doorstep.

42

The US Must Guard Against a Jean Charles de Menezes Disaster After Boston

Now that the FBI has published images of two suspects in the bombing of the Boston marathon, many people living in London, UK, will anxiously recall the disastrous actions of the Metropolitan Police in the aftermath of the terrorist 39. attacks on the London Underground in July 2005.

On 07 July, 2005, fifty-two people died following three suicide bomb attacks on the tube, and one on a London double decker bus. This was four years after the attacks in New York, but the world was still on high alert and in fear of further terror held to be in the name of Islam, by the perpetrators. The hunt for Osama Bin Laden was at its peak, as was George Bush's war on terror. Despite this, the Metropolitan Police Authority expressed an admirably moderate and reasoned approach in its statement on 08 July 2005:

"Reassurance is now a key word. The Authority is working with the Met to ensure that there is no backlash against particular communities. MPA members have been liaising with their link borough commanders to reassure communities whose members may feel vulnerable that we take their concerns seriously and are making every effort to prevent acts of recrimination. Extra patrols are on the beat in some areas and meetings are planned with local groups to spread the message. This is a vital job and we offer our full support."

The sub-text here is that the as London was a very diverse community, with many visible ethnic minorities, including many from Muslim backgrounds, who now found themselves at increased risk from others, as paranoia grew after 07 July. The term 'home-grown terrorists' was increasingly causing British Asians to become the target of suspicion, and abuse. Youth started using the term 'Bin Laden' or 'Osama' as terms of abuse for Asian youths.

On 21 July, there were four further attempted bombings on the London Underground, the devices failed and the would-be killers escaped into the general population. London was a very tense place to be, people became more edgy.

Soon, the images of the suspects, captured on CCTV, were soon all over the news network as the Metropolitan Police launched its largest ever manhunt. They proved woefully inadequate for the task, when on 22 July, officers followed a 27 year old Brazilian man living in London, Jean Charles de Menezes, into the underground at Stockwell station, and in front of terrified passengers, they immobilised him and pumped seven bullets into his head. The man, an electrician, was innocent, and completely unconnected to the offences. His only crime was to be vaguely of Islamic appearance and in the wrong place at the wrong time.

Although the de Menezes family, poor and with limited resources, living in Brazil at the time of the killing, they spent years seeking justice. No criminal charge was brought against any police officer, and an unlawful killing verdict was rejected in favour of an open verdict. The Metropolitan Police, as a corporate body, was fined having been found guilty under Health and Safety legislation.

The US regards the 2001 New York attacks as an act of war, by an international enemy. Obama is to be praised for his moderate rhetoric, and decision to address an Interfaith service for the victims signalling that he will not sanction the condemnation of an individual faith should it be shown that the perpetrators associate themselves with one religion.

43

What is Thatcher's Legacy to Black and Ethnic Minority People in the UK?

In the 1970s, Black and Ethnic Minority (BAME) people were treated as aliens in a UK that claimed to be tolerant to immigrants and racism was overt, and largely socially acceptable. Enoch Powell's overseas recruitment policy was to bring English speaking immigrants from the Commonwealth and Pakistan, to re-build the infrastructure of post war Britain, and to staff the developing National Health Service, and welfare services. The crippling recession of the 1980s, and high unemployment, soon brought simmering resentment of white working class, poor British people who felt BAME people were taking their jobs, housing, and public services. Soon, African and Caribbean families found themselves the victims of brutal attacks at the hands of members of flourishing of political organisations, such as the National Front, formed specifically to end and reverse black immigration to the UK. The police, rampant in their use of the hated SUS law, made the situation worse.

Thatcher's stance in 1978 was to condone, and empathise with public fears around black immigration, warning that people would feel 'swamped', the British character would be lost, and that the white British public would be hostile to those coming in from the Commonwealth and Pakistan. In her interview for Granada TV, 1978, she said:

"But there was a committee which looked at it and said that if we went on as we are then by the end of the century there would be four million people of the new Commonwealth or Pakistan here. Now, that is an awful lot and I think it means that people are really rather afraid that this country might be rather swamped by people with a different culture and, you know, the British character has done so much for democracy, for law and done so much throughout the world that if there is any fear that it might be swamped people are going to react and be rather hostile to those coming in".

Following this speech, her popularity soared, she was elected as Prime Minister the following year, and two years later, Britain's inner cities were burning. Her hardline stance on race and immigration was reflected in her contemplation of arming the police to quell rioters.

It was during her period in office that BAME people will be acutely aware of the consequences of politicians stoking up racial hatred, through use of coercive policing (and the hated Special Patrol Group will never be forgotten). She continued to maintain a position that was openly ambivalent about black immigration. Her private papers show, retrospectively, how strong her objection to BAME immigration, while feeling that white immigration would not be a problem. She wanted to prevent any Asian immigrants being given access to council housing, ahead of white people, particularly when faced with the prospect of having to house an expected influx of white Rhodesians, following the establishment of majority rule in Zimbabwe.

So, along with the trade unions, poor white working class people, mining and industrial communities in the north of England, do not forget the terrible legacy of xenophobia Thatcher bequeathed today's society and her political successors. Cameron certainly has not failed to learn her lessons.

44

Does Ed Miliband's Defeat of His Brother Signal the Type of PM He Will Make?

Younger siblings always want what the elder has; this is a common dynamic, universally observed to be part of family life. It starts with a glance at big brother's more exciting toys and games and finding them more attractive. Later his clothes, phone, and other possessions, appear more appealing particularly when what he has is always new, and the younger child's are inevitably hand-me-downs, less advanced or sophisticated.

But there are red lines, lines in the sand that are not to be crossed, even by the most distant siblings. This would include wanting and taking a sibling's partner or spouse, and ultimately, applying for the same job as your sibling. A woman I once worked with had made a pact with her sister never to work for the same organisation at the same time. It meant they could develop their individuality, and ultimately be at their competitive best without risk of hurting each other, or their families. It kept them close, gave them a common ground, and something which pulled them together. Looking at the Miliband family drama, the brothers should have possibly had the foresight to draw up such an agreement. But with such a father as the eminent Ralph Miliband, there was only ever one prize worth having. David, as the elder brother, inevitably would have assumed this was his birthright, and that Ed would have also tacitly understood that. But Ed tore up that script, and the story did not end satisfactorily for David, his many supporters in the party.

Those around them must have seen that the two ambitious and talented brothers, close in age, and following the same career trajectory, would have a collision at some point. Possibly their mother, Marion Kozak, foresaw it, indeed dreaded it. By swimming in different rivers in the New Labour project, the Milibands, and others close to them, probably did see clear blue water between the two. With David firmly aligned to Blair, and Ed in the Gordon Brown stream, their political fates were sealed by that aspect of their difference. By the time Gordon Brown was in the final year of his term of office, it was clear for all to see what a huge mistake it was for Blair to have been ousted, and replaced by a man who was leading them to an inevitable descent to defeat in 2010.

By this time, the brothers were so immersed in their political careers that their familial relationship became secondary. They were colleagues, in rival camps, and with a growing ideological gulf between them, brotherly love came a poor second. By the time of the Labour leadership elections, the fact of their kin relationship was incidental, and inconvenient. Others around them would have felt greater discomfort of the fact of the competition between the two of them. It was less important that they were brothers, and more important that they got the 'top job'. David's pain of losing the leadership, I suspect, would have been acute had he lost to Ed Balls, or Andy Burnham. But losing to his little brother introduced an added element that must have felt like a betrayal, a stolen birthright.

The story does not end with David deciding to move abroad, to lead respected charity International Rescue Committee, because even if he never returns to British politics, the failure of this dream will be a lifelong regret, and his brother a permanent reminder of it. Many, including this writer, found Ed much less convincing and talented than David, so if he does become the British prime minister, we know he will be a leader who is not sentimental about personal relationships, but will focus on what is necessary to achieve his achieve political goals.

45

Is Hillary Clinton Too Old to Be the Next President of the USA?

When leaving her State Department role this month, Hillary Clinton deservedly received many plaudits about her impact over the past four years. She will now be stepping off the political stage, but many believe this will only be for a short time while she reflects on her options. At the top of the list, she will be considering whether to run for the top job - the presidency. She will be 73 years old at the end of the next presidential term of office, and should she decide to run, her age is likely to be one of the main talking points. She can be expected to face questions about gun control, international terrorism, the economy, and even Benghazi, and answer them all with aplomb. But to deal effectively with the question of her age, she will need to develop an early strategy.

World leaders are getting younger, and even in America, they have not had an 'old' president since Ronald Reagan, who was 69 when he took office, the same age Hillary will be if she is elected. Back then, in 1980, the world was more middle aged and expected our leaders to have the gravitas and credibility that age can bring. Reagan was almost 78 when he left his second term of office. However, the arrival of Bill Clinton gave the world an expectation of not only younger leaders, but was also youthful ones. Since then, for Putin, Blair, Sarkozy, Obama and Cameron, being seen jogging played a part of their image as leaders.

When the personal factors of the future US presidential candidates are being debated, it is the fact that Hillary is a woman which should be the talking point, and how fantastic it would be to continue progress at the top of American politics for a woman to take the baton from an African American man. Whilst her enemies may not go to the extent of forming a campaign group in order to demand the publication of her health report, in the way they did to see Obama's birth certificate, they will be preoccupied with evidence of her vigour.

While an older man is seen as symbolising wisdom and credibility, the older woman is still associated with kindliness, and nurturing, not characteristics highly valued in international political leadership roles. Indeed, Hillary's strength and energy were defining characteristics of her time as secretary of state. It was frequently reported that she clocked up more air miles than any previous secretary of state. Perhaps it was already on her mind that she has to push herself to the edge, to prove her capabilities as a leader who is also an older woman.

Dealing with 'personality' questions is challenging for politicians, and the last thing they must do is to appear riled when these are asked. The stock approaches include straight rejection of the question and an insistence on addressing the real issues; use of humour to laugh off awkward personal questions; or accept the characteristic but cast a positive light on it so it is seen as an attribute. Ed Miliband moved through all of these stages with the 'Wallace' issue.

To be clear, Hillary must be permitted to run, if she chooses to, without hindrance of ageism or sexism. Of course, most references in quality debates will only allude to her age obliquely with references to her health or energy levels, and Hillary must rise above it and prove herself, as she is undoubtedly capable of.

46

How a subtle change in the NHS will turn patients into customers

The Government is introducing a change to the NHS that seeks to turn hospital patients into customers by asking them to take a loyalty test from April next year. It is one of many new NHS schemes intended to groom patients to think of hospitals as businesses.

We are used to being asked for feedback after shopping, going to a restaurant, or using a call centre. From next April, if you attend an A&E department, or have an overnight stay in hospital this will also be your experience. Before you leave, you will find yourself shepherded to an electronic device such as a kiosk, or tablet to tap out your experience.

You might be given a questionnaire or feedback card to complete before signing out. Or shortly after leaving hospital, you will get a text message, telephone call at home, or receive a postcard or questionnaire at home asking you to register your opinion.

Everyone knows that things can go seriously wrong in hospital care of patients, and patients have to be given ways of making their experience known. It is right to keep an eye on what patients are experiencing. That can be achieved without introducing a system that will ask patients to demonstrate their loyalty to a particular hospital by recommending it to others.

This is quite different from recommending a restaurant. Hospitals will be forced to ask discharged patients whether they would recommend a particular ward or A&E department to friends or family, if they needed similar care or treatment.

Called the Friends and Family Test, it will be part of the NHS Contract which provides hospitals with their income so they could face financial penalties if they do not comply. Results of the test will be published nationally for all hospitals.

The Government has rushed to implement this under researched methodology, based on the Net Promoter Score developed by Frederick F. Reicheld (Harvard Business Review, 2003) as a technique to boost company growth by creating customer loyalty in business.

Simply, those customers who give high scores are 'promoters' who are likely to shop with the company again, and speak well about it to others. Those who give low scores are 'detractors' who will speak badly of the company to others, and are unlikely to return.

Then there are those in the middle, the 'passives' or 'neutrals' who are fairly satisfied with the service, but will probably go elsewhere if they find something better.

A pilot at NHS Midlands and East has been operating this year, and publishes the results on their website, listing providers in order of performance.

Do we really use hospital services in the same way as we choose mobile phones? Or is it as it looks, and the Government is taking another step in creating greater market awareness in patients, pushing us further along the road to treating the NHS as a business. Let us hope NHS loyalty cards are not looming.

Reader comments:

Shrugged...

No, we don't choose hospitals like mobile phones but we are paying customers, albeit indirectly. Surely any organisation that wants to improve its service would want to solicit feedback.

The notion that 'patients are customers' was a product of Thatcherism and NHS staff were then told to find other terms to address the 'patients' – 'clients' became popular, service-user is the current term used in the mental health services on the basis that a client or customer usually chooses to purchase goods/services, but with detained service-users, it wasn't appropriate to use a term that suggests individual choice.

Not sure what teachers now call their pupils/students, but considering much of health care and education is not a choice it has always seemed strange to me that a market analogy is being used. And, of course, the power balance created by the conditions of any interaction with health care professionals really does not foster the idea that 'the customer is king'

Public sector worker objects to public feedback. Who knew?!

Shrugged. I pay for a service. Can steveb please explain why I'm not a customer?

And healthcare is a choice. I could choose to go private, or go to Romania or the US. Foreigners choose to come here. Americans have their teeth fixed in Mexico. Have you not heard of Health Tourism?

Hospitals make a habit of treating everyone who uses them as badly as they possibly can. The chance to give feedback is a great idea.

In principle this is a good idea – we need to ensure that there is a warning system about problems in patient care for government/managers to identify issues before they lead to patients dying. Such a system may well have identified mid staffs earlier.

However it does also need to be combined with protection for whistleblowers, greater advocacy services, and resources for staff so that instances such as hospitals running out of clean linen don't happen. The proposals described here are flawed. Often people who are mistreated will not speak up whist in hospital, so asking them to complete surevys in the very same building is self evidently flawed. Secondly, patient relatives should also be included. Finally, it goes without saying that such research should be conducted by people who know what they are doing. There is an awful lot of meaningless crap in market research, and these proposals could simply end up being used as PR tools for the companies involved knowing the media never question research methodology etc.

When I worked at the DWP on the DLA/AA section there was a push to call claimants 'customers', so it's not an unexpected move, and likely reflects the ideology of senior civil servants nicely.

Strawman alert.

 If you took more notice of what I have written, I was refer-ring to those services where the 'customer' had no choice to 'consume' certain services, and that is much of health, edu-cation and social care. The absolute foundation of a market is 'free entry and exit', when we have a law which forces us to participate, it is incongruent with a market situation. What kind of feed-back would you expect from persons who have been forced to take treatment against their will?

 Well said

 Erm, we don't have much of a choice whether to eat or not, do we?

 Having Healthcare free at the point of use is tremendously civilised, however there is a dark flip-side:

a) The providers can appear rather resentful or hostile towards patients (after all, they've already been paid so each new patient is a nuisance).

b) The users don't value or respect the service as they should, because it's "free".

Both attitudes are fairly basic aspects of human nature. Any attempt to square this circle ought to be encouraged, though it would be nice to see the providers more involved in how this should work. Otherwise, the unimpeachable ones may feel they're being poked with a stick.

 "(after all, they've already been paid so each new patient is a nuisance)."

Technically speaking, in England, they don't. They get paid per procedure. So the incentive here is to treat as many patients as possible for the shortest amount of time. In Wales the payment system is different, but it is still the case that each unit needs to treat a certain number of patients in order to meet royal college guidelines, otherwise the unit will probably be merged with others in a larger hospital.

So basically your wrong. Each additional patient is good news for a hospital.

"I was referring to those services where the 'customer' had no choice to 'consume' certain services, and that is much of health, education and social care."

In recent decades, we have recovered some choices in education (bog-standard comp, academy, free school or private, private with bursary etc), health (private or some increasing choice of NHS hospitals) and social care (state, charity or combination + buy-in of personal care). And, surely, choice must be extended further in public services – against the whinging of the provider interests!

"The absolute foundation of a market is 'free entry and exit', when we have a law which forces us to participate, it is incongruent with a market situation."

As usual, you are deeply muddled, steve. Free(er) markets admit of degree. No-one is "forced" to participate in state or private provision, despite the fantasies of authoritarian socialists who would abolish private medicine and education in favour of a 'Trabant/Skoda' healthcare and schooling for all.... Though, that said, many are now faced with accepting poor quality public services – think of Anne Clwyd's husband dying neglected in our "caring" NHS. The NHS and our education system are currently a national disgrace: they can be improved only by introducing more customer feedback and by judiciously involving more private but state-funded providers.

"What kind of feed-back would you expect from persons who have been forced to take treatment against their will?"

But no-one has been "forced" to take treatment against their will. Faced with a sub-standard NHS service, most accept what is available (believing, mistakenly, that it is the best), while others go private. Social 'democrats' and 'democratic' socialists seem to want less customer-responsive service in health and education: the state knows best, so take what you are given...? And, please, don't pull the 'libertarian socialist' utopia jag: we've been there, it won't happen and/because it is a contradiction in terms.

"Having Healthcare free at the point of use is tremendously civilised, however there is a dark flip-side:

a) The providers can appear rather resentful or hostile towards patients (after all, they've already been paid so each new patient is a nuisance).

b) The users don't value or respect the service as they should, because it's 'free'"

Exactly! Regarding (a), the solution is surely to make hospitals more customer-focussed and less provider-led by judicious privatisation and better management... Anecdote alert – (i) I recently visited (on my NHS consultant's advice) a private hospital for a £500 cancer test that the NHS does not provide. The service was superb: everyone made eye contact,was polite and made me feel welcome (even the cleaners), and none of the nurses were uncaring, waddling lard-arses. And (ii) I have had 4 elderly relatives die in NHS hospitals in different parts of the UK, and 3 died in appalling circumstances of neglect.

Regarding (b), agreed – just as, before prescription charges, people would visit the doctor for a 'free' prescription for elastoplast, paracetamol etc. This, and 'health tourism', suggest that minimum charges should be imposed, as on the continent. These could be automatically refunded to claimants, and many other problems could be covered by private insurance schemes with state supplements (as in France – widely regarded as the best health-care system in the world).

The results of any such hospital surveys are biased. Patients who died as the result of medical and care errors aren't able to respond.

BBC: How safe are our hospitals:
http://www.bbc.co.uk/iplayer/episode/b01p4wmx/Panorama_How_Safe_is_Your_Hospital/

This problem of treatment errors and care failings isn't new – it goes back to when New Labour was in government:

More than 3,000 hospital patients have died because of errors by NHS staff in England over the past year, figures show.

Hospitals reported 3,645 deaths in 2007-8 from patient safety incidents, data from the Lib Dems showed. [BBC website: 5 January 2009]

Point taken, though in my defence I was generalising to make a wider point.

After all, a particular nurse, for example, on a particular day will probably not be much driven (on a personal level) by the overall target.

I'm not seeking to criticise either healthcare workers or patients, though I think it reasonable to say that some on both sides are negatively affected for the reasons I suggest.

I can speak from personal experience of NHS hospital errors. Shortly before a scheduled hip operation in October 2010, I was presented with a surgery consent form with the wrong hip on it. Similar errors are surprisingly common:

– A toddler who fractured her leg was sent home with a plaster cast – on the wrong limb. Lucy Rylatt hobbled on the broken leg for five days before her parents realised the mistake. [Metro July 2012] – A doctor who removed the wrong fallopian tube from a patient, leaving her unable to conceive naturally, has been allowed to continue practising. A tribunal criticised Dr Samina Tahseen for her "hasty, careless and dismissive" treatment of the woman at Royal Derby Hospital in 2010.
The Medical Practitioners Tribunal Service panel found this amounted to "serious misconduct".
"There is now no possibility that Patient A will be able to conceive naturally"
But they decided she could continue to practise if she is supervised. [BBC 16 August 2012]

– A surgeon is waiting to learn if he will be struck off for removing a healthy kidney instead of a cancerous one from a patient in Ayrshire. Riza Murat Gurun admitted carrying out the operation at Ayr Hospital in 2006 without checking John Heron's scans. He has also admitted charges in relation to two other patients, one of whom died shortly after surgery. [BBC website February 2010]

Do we really use hospital services in the same way as we choose mobile phones?

Quite simply, yes we do. Customer choice driven through performance will improve standards as a whole through competition. Who in their right mind would choose a poor hospital unless they are forced to. If you have the choice between a good hospital and a poor one, you'll choose the good one if you can – especially if it is something as important as healthcare.

"Who in their right mind would choose a poor hospital unless they are forced to. If you have the choice between a good hospital and a poor one, you'll choose the good one if you can – especially if it is something as important as healthcare."

C'mon. In reality, patients often have little effective choice about which hospital they go to and virtually none in A&E cases. In most cases, the choice comes down to going to the nearest hospital with the relevant facilities.

I've responded to several official NHS post-op surveys which amount to no more than tick-box questionnaires. In responding, I've sometimes included an unsolicited note with written comments but I suspect that is unusual and, probably, unwelcome.

Is anyone keeping tabs on the amounts being paid out by the NHS in compensation for treatment errors and care failings?

"Who in their right mind would choose a poor hospital unless they are forced to"

If the poor hospital also offers a cheaper service (easyhospital type of thing. Dr Nick in the Simpsons) then it will easily survive in any form of market driven system. Health commissioners will pick it over the luxury hospital as it is cheaper, a private insurance company will do the same for the same reasons (except for customers who pick more expensive premiums), and private individuals who lack the income will probably take the chance. Lets consider the following example to illustrate this. Hospital A offers hip replacements for £5000, on average their success rate is 80% of operations last for 5 years. Hospital B offers hip replacements for £25,000 that last 8 years on average in 90% of cases.

Which hospital is going to get business from (a) a state funded body responsible for commissioning services?, (b) private insurance firms specialising in offering cheap premiums? and (c) Individuals not in the top 5% of earners?

And that's before we get into the information asymmetry that is inherent in the majority of healthcare systems. Hospital B may only be successful precisely because it has wealthy clients.

The concept of the 'customer' is a necessary development within a health system driven incrementally toward marketisation.

In time some 'customers' might be wealthy enough to afford deluxe health services (akin to flying business class, if we take a travel analogy) while the rest of us will just have to make do with Ryan-air.

When SERCO or VIRGIN are running hospitals they will be clean, uncrowded, and staff will always be smiling and helpful – there will even be policeman there to keep out the riff raff, just ask Wills, or Kate.

There is a highly successful market in healthcare in France is there not?

The state pays but (crucially) is not the monopoly provider. The patient chooses.

we can't afford it (and neither can the French nowadays).

The French system has ALWAYS cost more than the NHS – the cumulative difference must be astronomical.

As usual tories talk endlessly about choice (unless it is abortion) But they only really believe in choice for the rich. This is about changing the relationship between patient and hospital to one of customer. It is ideologically driven by the international right wing and is about turning health into just another commodity. Which for most people it is not. When you need emergency service you don't have either time to browse or travel to other areas. This data will be used to help flog off hospitals to the tory politicians corporate masters.

Anyone who has ever filled out any customer survey for gas or water or mobile phone or airline knows how pointless it is. The greatest myth in capitalism is that companies care about their customers. They don't. Capitalism is about giving the least possible service or product for the highest possible price.

Once health has been sold off the the real choice will set in. But you won't be choosing the hospital. The hospital will be choosing you.

 I'm sure they will have to make savings but I hardly think they are going to switch to the "envy of the world" state monopoly are they?!

 'I hardly think they are going to switch to the "envy of the world" state monopoly are they' – unlikely, that would require providing comparable outcomes at significantly lower GDP. Ignore the substantial difference in cumulative cost (over many decades) if it allows you to bang the same ideological drum

 With preventative surveys before treatment, rather than after, some costly treatments are preventable:

"An atlas published by the Government that maps variations in health spending and outcomes across England has highlighted some significant regional differences including amputation rates among diabetics. . . .

"Amputation rates among diabetics showed one of the most striking variations. Data revealed that the amputation rate for patients with Type 2 diabetes in the South West (3 in 1000 patients) is almost TWICE the rate in the South East. The Charity Diabetes UK was also concerned that the data showed less than half those with the disease (Types 1 and 2) had received nine key healthcare checks."

 there may be the sound of two drums!

 "Public sector worker objects to public feedback. Who knew?!"

 Brilliant comment. Adds so much to the debate. You are a genius.

"And (ii) I have had 4 elderly relatives die in NHS hospitals in different parts of the UK, and 3 died in appalling circumstances of neglect."
You let them die in neglect and did nothing, why didn't you pay for them to go private. Too busy down the pub Tony.

"Do we really use hospital services in the same way as we choose mobile phones?

Quite simply, yes we do. Customer choice driven through performance will improve standards as a whole through competition."

Quite simply, no we don't. If you get knocked down by a bus are you going to google "what's the best hospital for road accidents" and then make an informed decision before getting in a taxi ? Even if you could, what if that best hospital is at the other end of the country ?

My GP is the local GP. If I need to go to hospital I would choose the nearest one – believe it or not, people who are unwell generally don't want long journeys/unfamiliar cultures and would like visits from family/friends. "Choice" only works for elective/vanity surgery (enhancements, plastic surgery, etc) when there is real need and which shouldn't be provided by the state anyway.

Lastly, If choice works to drive up efficiency and standards, why hasn't it done it yet ? Both the tories in the early 90s and Blair a decade later, tried it, and it decreased productivity, more money in for decreasing output. Something Blair never understood was that to have choice you need an excess of supply over demand (which is why your local supermarket has a thousand lines of yoghurt) and public services always have the opposite (which is why the queue in your local A&E is longer than the one in the supermarket).

"Surely any organisation that wants to improve its service would want to solicit feedback".

What makes you think feedback = improved service ? Feedback is all part of the "customer services ethos" which is about allowing customers to think they are listened to and then carrying on providing the same shite service you always have whilst preserving the illusion of "choice". Virtually all private sector organisations ask for feedback and then take no notice of it – or are highly selective in how they interpret it. I'm sure lots of people gave negative feedback about being sold useless PPI, but banks did nothing until they were forced to by law. Lots of councils got negative feedback about fortnightly bin collections, and they are all still doing it, because it saves money. Who cares what the customer thinks ?

 I really can't see what's wrong with patient feedback. Yes the process may be flawed. Yes the results may be disregarded. But any system however inadequate which allows democratic input into the NHS must surely be a good thing.

 Without organised feedback systems to accommodate favourable responses from satisfied patients, unsolicited and unwelcome complaints will be the predominant form of feedback. Btw in large urban areas, patients often do have effective choices between hospitals for many elective treatments even though choice is limited or non-existent for acute cases and especially for A&E. In mainland Europe, hospitals and GPs manage to cope with competition although the same caveats apply as to the limited extent of competition between hospitals.

 But I'd be extremely surprised if the average NHS patient is using the service for elective surgery ? (Which means things like cosmetic surgery) Most people in NHS hospitals are there because a doctor has said they should be and increasingly the NHS is primarily used by an ageing population with multiple, chronic and long term health issues which are treatable but not curable. The bottom line is the NHS shouldn't be funding elective surgery, which is why it's absurd to argue it should offer "choice"

47

MPs are also partly to blame for the Mid-Staffs NHS Scandal

When Julie Bailey, founder of Cure the NHS (@curetheNHS) campaign group, contacted her local MP about the horrors at Mid Staffordshire NHS trust, to her great anger, she was invited to a Labour Party meeting instead.

The MP for Stafford between 1997 and 2010 was David Kidney (@davidkidney), the crucial period when patients suffered so grievously. He had extensive knowledge of the hospital, and even worked there during the Parliamentary summer recess to better understand the environment.

Ms Bailey wrote to him detailing her suffering of her mother who died at the hospital during this period, only to receive a very complacent response. The Francis Inquiry report states about Ms Bailey:

She felt that Mr Kidney's reply effectively denied the low standard of care evidenced by her and other constituents' experiences at the hospital.

Kidney isn't the only MP who came off poorly in the report, they were criticised for simply passing on complaints received from constituents back to the hospital. A year after she first made her complaint to Kidney, Ms Bailey and 30 members of her campaign group visited his surgery and individually described their awful experiences.

He responded by agreeing to arrange a meeting between the group and the hospital staff, the very organisation that had harmed them and their loved ones, then put up a wall of silence to their complaints.

MPs should have served their constituents better, and certainly not offered invitations to a party policy development group, at which their experiences would provide the Party with political leverage, but do nothing for patients and relatives. Ms Bailey was upset that her MP appeared to be using her suffering to further the work of his Party.

The inquiry report gently asks them to do better next time and deferentially asks them to consider developing systems to allow them to pick up on systematic organisational failure. Rightly, it acknowledges that MPs are not health regulators, but also point out they can be held to account by their electorate and should do better.

None of the local MPs, including David Kidney has been apportioned blame in the report, for after all, the damage was within hospital walls, but the report cites their parliamentary code of conduct for MPs:

Members have a general duty to act in the interests of the nation as a whole, and a special duty to their constituents.

There are clearly competing demands between the needs of the Party and the needs of constituents. This was a situation where the constituent's needs should have been paramount.

48

New Poll suggests UKiP to propel Labour to outright victory in 2015

With widespread predictions of another hung parliament in the 2015 general elections in the UK, attention has focused on the role of the Liberal Democrats as kingmakers once again. However, a new poll suggests that Labour could win an outright majority due to predicted strong performance in the marginal seats. The report of the findings of the research funded by Tory peer Michael Ashcroft in Bloomberg follows on from earlier similar research published this year.

It is the due to predicted strong performance of UKip in 40 marginal Tory seats, as well as Labour's own showing in these marginals which is stronger than its performance overall in the polls in the country as a whole. Whilst Lord Ashcroft has no personal or political credibility among right thinking Labour supporters, this research is undoubtedly intended to galvanise the Tories to sign up to more right wing action.

This latest poll covers the period up to September 5, 2013 and comes at a time when Conservative Party is driving through a programme of welfare reform that attacks the most vulnerable with the bedroom tax, universal credit, child benefit, immigration bonds, racist 'go home' vans and the destruction of public services. It also comes at a time when Ukip strength is growing following the surge in support for the party at the 2013 local elections. Ukip's performance in the Eastleigh by-election this year, in which they beat the Conservatives, led to reassurance from David Cameron that the Tories would not respond by veering to the right.

The results of this new poll may be a 'call to arms' for the Tory party, to push for more radical right wing stance to prevent the march of Ukip in the marginals and prevent an outright Labour win. A Labour win in 2015, however, is crucial to reverse the trampling on the rights of the most vulnerable.

49

EU benefits are 'land grab' by Brussels, says Duncan Smith

The EU Commissioner for employment and social affairs, Laszlo Andor, is taking the British government to *court* over what it says are discriminatory practices in its application of regulations on welfare payments.

EU foreign nationals living in the UK are eligible to claim welfare benefits if they pass the qualifying tests. One of these is the test of 'habitual residence' which should be applied in the EU.

Instead, however, the UK requires EU nationals to pass a more challenging 'right to reside' test, which many fail.

Iain Duncan Smith, work and pensions secretary (pictured) has stated that Britain will *resist* this attempted "land grab" by Europe, in a bid to end "benefit tourism" to the UK.

In the run up to the next general election, and following a hypothetical outright Conservative election win, this represents a crucial battle for Tories. They have committed to an 'in/out' referendum in 2017 if attempts to win back powers from Brussels cannot be negotiated.

Curiously Nick Clegg has supported Duncan Smith's upcoming battle in the European Court of Justice, seeing it as protecting the UK welfare benefits system from becoming a "free for all".

EU nationals working in the UK have complained to the commissioner of having access to family welfare and unemployment benefits denied despite having the right to live and work in the UK. Duncan Smith can claim that Britain is not alone in finding the European welfare benefit rules unfair, as wealthier countries Holland, Austria and Germany have also challenged the rules.

Restrictions on the rights of EU national from Romania and Bulgaria will be lifted at the end of this year, fuelling fears that people from the more impoverished European nations could flock to the UK, or wealthier UK nations, to claim benefits.

50

The shocking death of Nigerian student in Durham Prison and the search for the truth

A Nigerian student, Boniface Umale, has died at Durham prison, shortly after his arrest. His death was only discovered when his visiting solicitor arrived at the jail to find arrangements being made for his cremation, according to *Nigerian Watch*.

A Nigerian student, Boniface Umale, has died at Durham prison, shortly after his arrest. His death was only discovered when his visiting solicitor arrived at the jail to find arrangements being made for his cremation, according to Nigerian Watch.

The 24 year old international student completed his first degree in 2008 at Northumbria University, Newcastle, and then embarked on a Master's Degree in engineering. He was arrested on 24 March and held in Durham prison. The circumstances surrounding his arrest and death are unknown to his family, and it is unclear whether he had been charged with any offence or was a remand prisoner.

More worryingly is the fact that arrangements were apparently made to cremate him without consulting his family, or the Nigerian High Commission, which has now been notified. Cremation is deemed to be culturally unacceptable and would add to the great distress to his family and community if conducted.

Prison death rates

This case highlights the need for a review of the care and treatment of prisoners at high risk of death in prisons, and a review of the safety issues in the management of foreign prisoners. The rates of prison deaths, for all prisoners in England and Wales, are unacceptably high.

The situation for foreign inmates in prisons in England and Wales worsens as their population grows to the rate of 13 per cent in

2012. The ethnicity of foreign prisoners is crucially important, as 62 per cent foreign prisoners in jails in England and Wales are from an ethnic minority group.

Home secretary Theresa May has set an aggressive policy stance towards foreign prisoners in her determination to secure an *unsympathetic* stance towards them. Are they treated equally and with fairness in prison, compared with others? It is unlikely. Public opinion on the *management* of offenders is very conservative, shunning the idea of votes for prisoners, strongly supporting the deportation of Abu Qatada irrespective of human rights legislation, and in favour of a repatriation of rights from the European Court.

Ministry of Justice *statistics* recording the percentage of all deaths in prison by ethnicity show high rates for black and ethnic minority prisoners, peaking at 18.5 per cent in 2007.

Family Appeal

Family spokesman and friend of Boniface, Daniel Okpla, has issued *an open letter* setting out concerns and unanswered questions in the case.

The facts of this case are yet to emerge. It is to be hoped that the family and friends of Boniface Umale will not only learn the truth, but will be treated with respect and dignity in the future handling of the case, which has been disturbingly lacking to date. More broadly, a review of the care and treatment of vulnerable foreign prisoners, particularly those from ethnic minority backgrounds, is warranted.

Reader comments:

 Isn't this using an individual's case for political purposes. I thought such acts were anathema to the left and only done by the right.

 I don't think there is anything particularly left wing about being honest with statistics. However, if you read the article above it clearly places Boniface Umale's death in the wider context of prison deaths across the UK. What's wrong with using an individual case study provided you don't use it to distort the overall picture?

No, you're right. It's not a particularly left wing about being honest with stats. The right wing do the same thing. However you are wrong about the honesty bit. Both sides are far from honest about their stats. They always use it to push their argument.

As to individual cases. They always distort the overall picture. Why? Because they are individual cases. If there was a common pattern and something that was happening frequently then it wouldn't be an individual case any more. But since an individual case is being used then it must be by definition something that is not common or frequent.

Be it individual cases like Mike Philpott's being used to tar the whole social security system or the case of Boniface Umale being used to counter the process of removing foreign prisoners from our jails, all individual cases lead to bad decisions and bad law. The phrase "hard cases makes for bad law" exists for a reason.

As for distorting. The story above mixes foreign prisoners with BME prisoners distorting the picture.

Thanks for sharing, It was nice reading this blog.

About the author

CLAUDIA TOMLINSON was born in London and has forged a career mainly in the health sector, and in adult education. A writer since childhood, she has published many articles, including blog articles, and is author of two published books. She has contributed to Left Foot Forward, Huffington Post UK, Liberal Conspiracy and the Independent.

.